Check and test

Science

**Morton Jenkins, Rod Clough,
Mary Whitehouse**

Published by BBC Educational Publishing,
BBC White City, 201 Wood Lane, London W12 7TS.

First published 2001 Reprinted september 2003

ISBN 0 563 54447 3

Illustrations by Hardlines Ltd

Reproduced by Spectrum Colour, England

Printed in Italy by Poligrafico Dehoniano

Contents

About GCSE Bitesize

GCSE Bitesize is a revision service designed to help you achieve success in your exams. There are books, television programmes and a website, which can be found at **www.bbc.co.uk/revision**. It's called *Bitesize* because it breaks revision into bite-sized chunks to make it easier to learn. *Check and Test* is the latest addition to the *Bitesize* revision service.

How to use this book

This book is divided into the 100 essential topics you need to know so your revision is quick and simple. It provides a quick test for each bite-sized chunk, so you can check that you know it!

Use this book to check your understanding of GCSE Science. If you can prove to yourself that you're confident with these key ideas, you'll know that you're on track with your learning.

You can use this book to test yourself:

- during your GCSE course
- at the end of the course during revision.

As you revise you can use *Check and Test* in several ways:

- as a summary of the essential information on each of the 100 topics to help you revise those areas
- to check your revision progress: test yourself to see how confident you are with each topic
- to keep track and plan your time: you can aim to check and test a set number of topics each time you revise, knowing how many you need to cover in total and how much time you've got.

GCSE Bitesize revision materials

GCSE Bitesize Revision: Science is a book which contains the key information and skills you need to revise, plus lots of tips and practice questions to help you improve your results (ISBN: 0 563 46120 9).

The *GCSE Bitesize Revision: Science* website provides even more practice and explanation to help you revise. It can be found at **www.bbc.co.uk/revision**.

The Science exam

There are two levels of Science examination: Foundation Tier and Higher Tier. This book covers both levels. Higher papers are marked with a **h** logo in the margin. Your school or college will determine which tier is best for you, and your teacher will usually discuss this with you before your entry is sent to the Board.

Most exam questions are based on two main types of question:

1 there are simple questions, where you may be asked to define a key term, give an example or do an easy calculation

2 there are questions where you have to apply your knowledge.

In Higher Tier papers you are also asked open-ended questions. These questions often start with words such as 'Explain' or 'Discuss'. The number of lines in the answer booklet gives an indication of the length of answer required.

Always read the questions carefully to see exactly what they mean. If you are pressed for time, give shorter answers to all the questions rather than long answers to only the easy ones. In that way, you will gain more marks!

Good luck!

BBC GCSE Check and Test: Science

Life processes and cell activity

Check the facts

> A **cell** is the basic unit of structure of all living organisms, excluding **viruses**.

All living cells have a mixture of chemicals, called **cytoplasm**, and a membrane, which controls the entry and exit of substances.

Most living cells have a **nucleus**, which controls all the activities within the cell, such as **cell division**. Exceptions include red blood cells in mammals.

The main differences between plant and animal cells are that plant cells have a non-living **cellulose cell wall** surrounding the **cell membrane** and, when mature, have a large vacuole inside them containing **cell sap**.

Many plant cells in leaves and stems also contain **chloroplasts** for **photosynthesis**.

Test yourself

The diagram shows two types of cell:

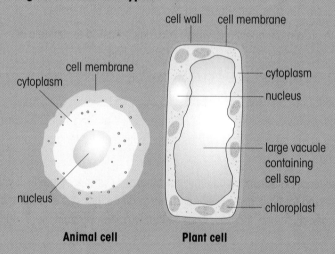

Animal cell   Plant cell

1 State the function of:
   a) the chloroplast
   b) the nucleus
   c) the cell membrane.

2 Name three structures, visible in the diagram, which only occur in plant cells.

3 Name a type of animal cell which does not have a nucleus.

Check the facts

All cells are produced from pre-existing cells by cell division.

Chromosomes in a nucleus are needed before cell division can take place.

There are two main types of cell division:

Mitosis produces two identical daughter cells from an original parent cell and is responsible for growth and repair of tissues.

Meiosis occurs only in the production of reproductive cells. For every one cell that divides in this way four daughter cells are produced (each with half the normal number of chromosomes). Eggs and sperm are made by meiosis.

h

Test yourself

1 Name the type of cell division which is responsible for the production of:
a) new skin cells when they are worn away
b) sperm.

2 If there are 46 chromosomes in a normal body cell, how many would there be in an egg?

3 Name a structure in a cell which must be present before cell division can take place.

4 The diagram shows a stage in mitosis.

Name the structures A and B.

h

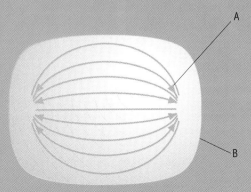

Life processes and cell activity

BBC GCSE Check and Test: Science

Check the facts

**Respiration is the process which releases
energy from glucose in all living cells.**

Aerobic respiration takes place when oxygen is present. It is responsible for the complete breakdown of glucose, with the release of much more energy than when oxygen is not used.

Water and carbon dioxide are the waste products:

glucose + oxygen → carbon dioxide + water

In **anaerobic respiration** in yeast, a little energy is released. Ethanol and carbon dioxide are the waste products.

Some bacteria in milk respire anaerobically and make **lactic acid**. When we exercise vigorously, our muscle cells behave in a similar way.

Test yourself

A very simplified diagram showing different forms of respiration

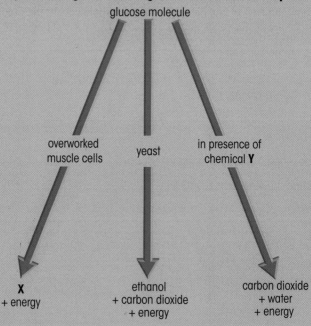

1 Name product X.

2 Name the chemical represented by Y.

3 Name a commercial product which can be made by respiring yeast.

Life processes and cell activity

www.bbc.co.uk/revision

Check the facts

Diffusion is the random movement of molecules, moving from a region of high concentration to one of low concentration.

Osmosis is a form of diffusion which involves only the movement of water molecules.

Osmosis is the movement of water from where it is in high concentration to where it is in low concentration, through a semi-permeable membrane, until there is an even concentration of molecules.

Cell membranes are **semi-permeable**.

Test yourself

Section through a root hair cell

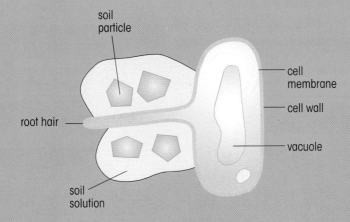

soil particle

cell membrane

cell wall

root hair

vacuole

soil solution

1 a) State two differences between the terms diffusion and osmosis.

b) Explain why water passes from the soil solution into the root hair.

2 Suggest why most plants die if salt water is added to the soil in which they grow.

3 Describe another situation where osmosis takes place in living organisms.

Check the facts

Gas exchange in the lungs depends on movement of air in and out of the thorax (chest).

Breathing in

During **inhalation** the rib cage moves upwards and outwards, while the diaphragm contracts, becoming flattened rather than dome shaped.

Inhalation results in an increase in volume of the thorax with a decrease in pressure compared with **atmospheric pressure** so that air rushes into the lungs.

Breathing out

During **exhalation** the rib cage moves downwards and inwards, the diaphragm relaxes and becomes dome shaped and the air is forced out due to an increase in pressure helped by the recoil of the elastic lungs.

Test yourself

The position of the ribs and diaphragm during inhalation and exhalation

Side view of thorax (chest)

A Inhalation (breathing in)   B Exhalation (breathing out)

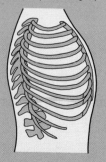
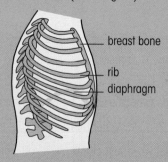

breast bone

rib
diaphragm

1 State two visible differences between the ribs and diaphragm in A and B.

2 Complete the following statements using the following words to help:

increases	decreases	stays the same

a) During exhalation the volume of the thorax _____

b) During exhalation the pressure in the lungs _____.

Check the facts

Oxygen debt occurs when an aerobically respiring animal has to respire anaerobically due to a temporary shortage of oxygen.

If the demand for oxygen in muscle cells exceeds the supply, muscles respire anaerobically for a short time.

h This releases some energy, but results in a build-up of lactic acid in the blood.

Example

This is the case during 'quick burst' activities, such as sprinting. At the end of the sudden exercise the lactic acid needs to be broken down aerobically – the athlete breathes heavily to obtain the oxygen needed for this, which is called the oxygen debt.

Test yourself

1 Name the type of respiration that does not need oxygen.

2 The table shows a comparison between two athletes who ran races of different distances.

Athlete	A	B
Distance of race (m)	100	10 000
Oxygen needed (dm^3)	10	150
Oxygen entering blood (dm^3)	0.5	134.0

h

The difference between the oxygen needed and the oxygen actually entering the blood during the race is called the oxygen debt.

a) What is the oxygen debt for each of the athletes?

b) When the race is over, both athletes continue to breathe more deeply than normal for some time. Explain the reason for this.

3 Write a word equation for the anaerobic respiration taking place in the muscles of an athlete with a large oxygen debt.

Humans as organisms

Check the facts

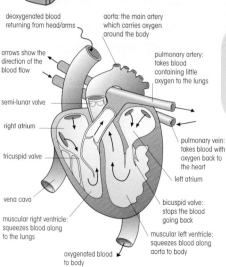

deoxygenated blood returning from head/arms

aorta: the main artery which carries oxygen around the body

arrows show the direction of the blood flow

pulmonary artery: takes blood containing little oxygen to the lungs

semi-lunar valve

right atrium

pulmonary vein: takes blood with oxygen back to the heart

tricuspid valve

left atrium

vena cava

bicuspid valve: stops the blood going back

muscular right ventricle: squeezes blood along to the lungs

muscular left ventricle: squeezes blood along aorta to body

oxygenated blood to body

In mammals the heart consists of four chambers (two upper atria and two lower ventricles) with the left and right sides totally separate.

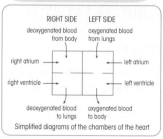

RIGHT SIDE	LEFT SIDE
deoxygenated blood from body	oxygenated blood from lungs
right atrium →	← left atrium
right ventricle →	← left ventricle
deoxygenated blood to lungs	oxygenated blood to body

Simplified diagrams of the chambers of the heart

Deoxygenated blood is carried to the right atrium via the **vena cava**. Oxygenated blood from the lungs goes to the left atrium in the **pulmonary vein**. The blood passes into the ventricles through valves, which prevent back-flow. Contraction of the ventricles forces oxygenated blood around the body via the aorta and deoxygenated blood to the lungs via the pulmonary arteries. Remember: diagrams of the heart are shown as if you are looking at someone else's chest, so if the left side is on the right and vice versa.

Test yourself

1 Suggest why the wall of the left ventricle is more muscular than the wall of the right ventricle.

2 State the function of the valves between the atria and the ventricles.

3 Students measured their pulse rates when sitting and after exercise:

Activity	Pulse rate
	(beats per minute)
Sitting in a chair	70
After running up and down the stairs	130
2 minutes later	100
10 minutes later	70

a) Explain the results.

b) Give another factor which would have its rate affected by this exercise.

c) Afterwards, one student's face was red. Explain the advantage of this.

Check the facts

Enzymes are proteins made by living organisms. They speed up the rate of chemical reactions, i.e. they are catalysts.

They can be taken out of cells and used as extracts in products, such as washing powders. They work only in a narrow range of temperatures and pH values.

They are **denatured** (destroyed) when they are boiled.

Each enzyme catalyses a particular reaction. Some help in building large molecules from small ones; others, like digestive enzymes, break large molecules into smaller ones.

Test yourself

1 Define an enzyme.

Hydrogen peroxide is a waste material produced in cells. It is poisonous and so is broken down into water and oxygen by an enzyme called catalase. Three different tissues were investigated as follows:

Three measuring cylinders were set up, each with 12 cm³ of hydrogen peroxide and some washing up liquid. A 1 cm³ piece of each tissue was placed in each of three measuring cylinders. Bubbles of froth were formed and, at the end of three minutes, the volume of froth was recorded.

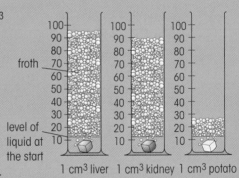

1 cm³ liver   1 cm³ kidney   1 cm³ potato

2 Look at the diagram and then answer these questions:

a) Which type of tissue contained the most catalase?

b) Explain your answer.

3 State two other factors which must be kept constant to make it a 'fair test'.

4 What would happen if boiled liver was used instead?

5 Explain why it would be a good idea to repeat the experiment several times to calculate the average volume of froth for each tissue.

Humans as organisms

BBC GCSE Check and Test: Science

Check the facts

Humans as organisms

Insulin is a hormone that controls the concentration of glucose in the blood.

Glucose is maintained at a concentration of $0.1\,g$ per $100\,cm^3$ of blood.

Lack of insulin leads to **diabetes** (the inability to regulate blood sugar).

Insulin is made by special cells in the **pancreas**.

Its secretion into the blood stream is stimulated by high concentrations of glucose in the blood, such as are found after a meal.

Insulin stimulates excess glucose to be changed into **glycogen**, which is stored in the liver and muscles.

Test yourself

1 Explain the function of insulin.

2 There are two types of diabetes:

> **Type 1:** This person produces little or no insulin.
> Daily injections of insulin are needed.
>
> **Type 2:** This person produces a lower than normal amount of insulin.
> Daily injections of insulin are not needed.

Suggest how a person with type 2 diabetes may control the disease.

3 The graph shows how the amount of insulin produced by untreated sufferers of each type of diabetes changes during a 12-hour period.

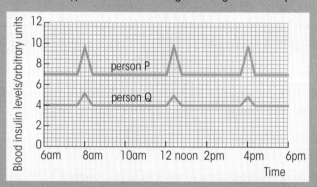

a) Which person has type 2 diabetes?

b) Suggest why the amounts of insulin increase in both graphs at certain times during the 12-hour period.

Check the facts

Sex hormones cause the development of secondary sexual characteristics at the time of puberty.

In females, the secondary sexual characteristics include menstruation, breast development, broadening hips and growing pubic and armpit hair.

In males, at puberty there is a deepening of the voice, increased growth of body hair and a general increase in muscle development.

Certain cells in the ovaries and testes produce sex hormones.

Ovaries secrete the female sex hormones, **oestrogen** and **progesterone**.

Oestrogen	Progesterone
Promotes ripening of the egg and starts the thickening of the uterus lining.	Maintains the growth of the lining of the uterus.

The testes produce the male sex hormone called **testosterone**.

Test yourself

1 State the name of the male sex hormone.

2 Where in the body is this hormone made?

3 The graph shows the production of male sex hormone in relation to age.

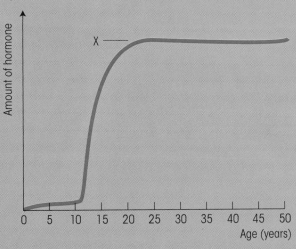

What is the term used to describe the changes to the body at point X on the graph?

4 List the expected effects of this sex hormone on the development of males between the ages of fifteen and twenty.

Humans as organisms

BBC GCSE Check and Test: Science

Check the facts

Blood consists of red and white cells, and platelets suspended in a liquid called plasma.

The red blood cells contain **haemoglobin** to carry oxygen to all parts of the body.

The plasma carries **carbon dioxide** as sodium hydrogen carbonate from the cells to the lungs.

The plasma also carries **nutrients** and **hormones** to the cells, and **urea** as a waste product.

Some white blood cells engulf and digest bacteria, while others make antibodies for immunity.

Platelets help to clot the blood.

Test yourself

Some structures and processes taking place in a blood capillary

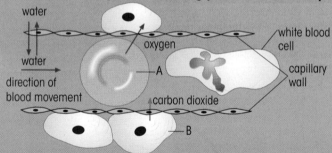

1 Name the type of cell labelled A.

2 Which part of the blood carries:
   a) glucose   b) oxygen   c) carbon dioxide?

3 State two differences you can see between the structure of cell A and the structure of cell B.

4 Name one substance other than oxygen that passes from the blood to the tissues.

5 State one example of diffusion shown in the diagram.

6 Give two ways that the blood cells defend the body against disease-causing organisms.

Check the facts

Absorption is the movement of digested food molecules through the small intestine wall into the blood system. Nutrients are carried to where they are needed in the body.

The lining of the small intestine is very thin and has its surface area increased by finger-like villi.

Villi are rich in **capillaries** to absorb glucose and amino acids.

They also have **lacteals** for the absorption of fat.

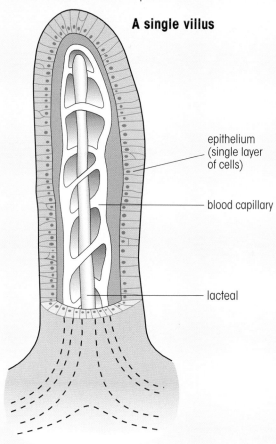

A single villus

epithelium (single layer of cells)

blood capillary

lacteal

Humans as organisms

Test yourself

1 In which part of the digestive system would you find villi?

2 How do the epithelium, blood capillary and lacteal in the diagram make the villus well-adapted to its function?

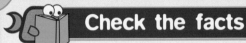

Check the facts

Digestion is the breakdown of large insoluble molecules of food into smaller soluble molecules, by **digestive enzymes**.

> **The digestive system consists of the alimentary canal and associated glands.**

The glands secrete digestive enzymes, breaking food down so that the nutrients can be absorbed into the blood system. **Carbohydrates**, such as starch, are broken down into simple sugars; **proteins** into amino acids; and **fats** into fatty acids and glycerol.

Food that is not digested passes out of the body at the anus.

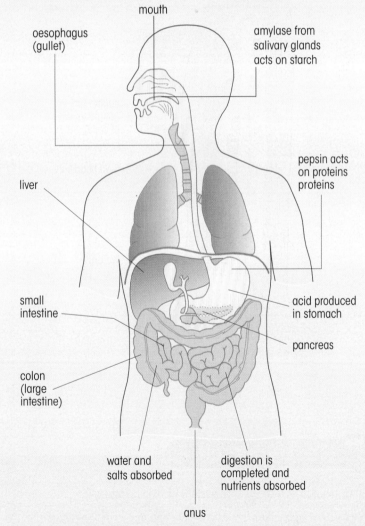

mouth

oesophagus (gullet)

amylase from salivary glands acts on starch

pepsin acts on proteins proteins

liver

small intestine

acid produced in stomach

pancreas

colon (large intestine)

water and salts absorbed

digestion is completed and nutrients absorbed

anus

h

Test yourself

1 Bile emulsifies fats (turns them into small droplets).
How will this help enzymes to digest fats?

2 State two things which need to happen to food before nutrients can be absorbed into the blood.

3 Name a place in the digestive system where:
   a) the contents are acidic
   b) amylase digests starch
   c) most water is absorbed from food.

4 Name an organ in the alimentary canal where the following enzymes work:
   a) pepsin
   b) amylase.

5 Study the graph and answer the following questions:

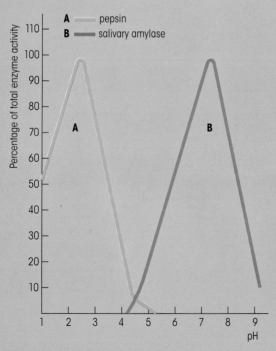

a) At what pH is pepsin most active?
b) Which enzyme has the widest range of activity?
c) Explain why both enzymes cannot work together in the same place.

Humans as organisms

Humans as organisms

Check the facts

The vertebrate eye is a spherical organ, connected to the brain by the optic nerve. It has an outer protective layer with a transparent front – the **cornea**. The outer coat is lined with a black layer, supplying the eye with blood. Muscles are used for adjusting the shape of the **lens** and the **iris**. In the centre of the iris is a hole – the **pupil**.

> **Light enters through the pupil, passes through the lens and reaches the light sensitive layer, called the retina. This contains receptor cells called rods and cones.**

Automatic focusing takes place during a process called accommodation. The eye focuses on near objects by contracting the **ciliary muscles**, slackening the **suspensory ligament**, making the lens more convex (fatter), and constricting the pupil. The eye focuses on distant objects by relaxing the ciliary muscles, stretching the suspensory ligament, making the lens less convex (thinner), and widening the pupil.

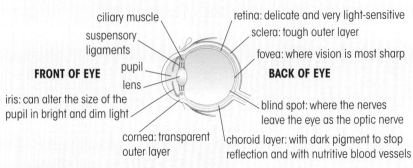

ciliary muscle
suspensory ligaments
FRONT OF EYE
pupil
lens
iris: can alter the size of the pupil in bright and dim light
cornea: transparent outer layer

retina: delicate and very light-sensitive
sclera: tough outer layer
fovea: where vision is most sharp
BACK OF EYE
blind spot: where the nerves leave the eye as the optic nerve
choroid layer: with dark pigment to stop reflection and with nutritive blood vessels

Test yourself

Look at the diagram of the front of a human eye. The distance (AB) across the pupil changes.

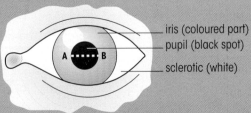

iris (coloured part)
pupil (black spot)
sclerotic (white)

1 Under what condition does the distance AB become smaller?

2 What is the advantage of being able to vary the size of the pupil?

3 The change in size of the pupil is a reflex action. Name one other reflex action performed by the eye and state its advantage.

4 Explain how the eye focuses on objects at different distances.

Check the facts

Reflex actions are involuntary, rapid responses to stimuli performed when electrical nerve impulses are generated from receptors.

The impulses pass along a sensory neurone from the receptor to a connecting (relay) neurone in the spinal cord. The impulse passes out via a motor neurone and on to the effector organ, which brings about a response.

Example

Sneezing, coughing, blinking and withdrawing your finger from a sharp object are all forms of reflex action.

Effectors are always muscles or glands. Most reflexes protect the body.

Test yourself

1 The diagram shows the path taken by a nervous impulse during a reflex action when a finger touches a drawing pin.

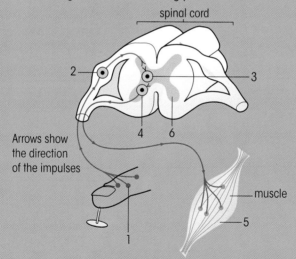

spinal cord

Arrows show the direction of the impulses

muscle

Choose six names from this list to identify the numbers on the diagram.

| effector | grey matter | motor neurone | relay neurone |
| sensory neurone | synapse | white matter | receptor |

2 What are the advantages of a reflex action?

3 We are able to detect changes in our surroundings. What is the term used to describe these changes?

4 Name four organs found in the body which can detect a change in our surroundings and state the change to which each might respond.

Humans as organisms

Check the facts

The kidneys control the chemical make-up of the blood by removing waste and regulating the blood's composition.

Each kidney has over one million tiny filters called **nephrons**.

There are two stages to removing waste from the blood:

•filtration

•reabsorption

Filtration

This takes place in a tiny knot of blood capillaries, called a **glomerulus**, which sits in the cup-like **Bowman's capsule** at the beginning of each nephron. Filtration occurs because the pressure of the blood forces small molecules through into the tubule. These include water and solutes, such as salts, glucose and urea.

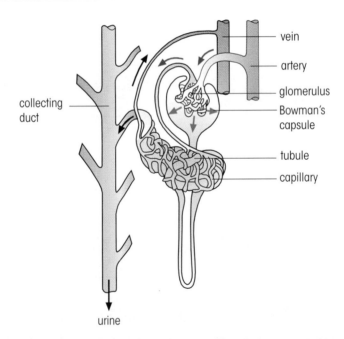

collecting duct

vein

artery

glomerulus

Bowman's capsule

tubule

capillary

urine

Reabsorption

Kidney tubules are parts of the nephrons that reabsorb useful materials.

At the end of each nephron, the waste product – urine – contains some of these solutes, while others have been reabsorbed back into the blood.

Urine passes from the kidney to the bladder.

Humans as organisms

www.bbc.co.uk/revision

Test yourself

1 State the function of the capillary.

2 State what causes blood to be filtered in the glomerulus.

3 The table shows the composition of the liquid in the glomerulus and in the collecting duct.

Substance	Glomerulus (g per cm³)	Collecting duct (g per cm³)
water	90.0	95.0
protein	8.0	0
urea	0.03	2.0
glucose	0.10	0
salts	0.42	1.18

a) Which substances have not passed into the collecting duct?

b) Suggest what has happened to these materials.

c) What can you deduce from the table about the functions of the kidneys?

4 Explain how filtration under pressure takes place in the Bowman's capsule.

Humans as organisms

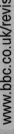

Humans as organisms

> **When blood is filtered through the walls of the blood capillaries in the kidney tubules, the filtrate contains some essential materials which the body cannot afford to lose:**
> • glucose   • amino acids   • mineral salts   • water

h

All of the glucose and amino acids are reabsorbed back into the blood capillaries which surround the tubules.

Water and **mineral salts**, which are needed by the body, are also reabsorbed into the capillaries surrounding the tubules.

The degree of water reabsorption is under the control of a hormone called **anti-diuretic hormone (ADH)**.

When there is little water in the blood, a lot of ADH and little urine is produced. When there is a lot of water in the blood, little ADH and a lot of urine is produced.

Test yourself

The composition of urine is regulated by the kidney tubules. The table shows information about the kidneys of three different mammals.

Mammal	Length of tubule (arbitrary units)	Concentration of urine
Beaver (lives in lakes)	1.3	dilute
Human	3.0	medium
Desert rat	10.4	very concentrated

h

1 How many times longer is the tubule of the desert rat compared with that of the beaver?

2 Explain how ADH controls the concentration of urine.

3 Why does a desert rat need to produce more concentrated urine than a beaver?

Check the facts

Skin **regulates your body temperature.**

On cold days:
- you shiver – the muscles under the skin contract and relax rapidly, thus generating heat
- the blood capillaries in the skin constrict so that very little blood reaches the skin and so less heat is radiated away
- the hairs on your skin stand up because the erector muscles contract; this traps a layer of insulating air between the hairs.

On hot days:
- you sweat – the skin is cooled when the sweat **evaporates** from its surface
- the blood vessels in your skin dilate so that more blood reaches the skin and excess heat is radiated from your body.

Humans as organisms

Test yourself

Some of the structures in human skin

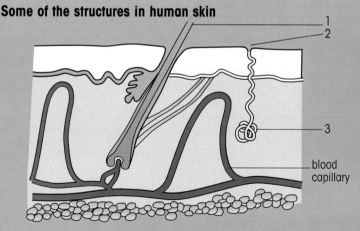

1
2
3
blood capillary

1 Name the parts labelled 1 to 3.

2 State what happens to the blood capillaries when the temperature outside is:
a) very low
b) very high.

3 State another way in which skin reacts to a rise in temperature.

4 Why does evaporation of sweat cool the body?

BBC GCSE Check and Test: Science

Check the facts

Photosynthesis is the series of chemical reactions in which **glucose** is made. Light energy is converted to chemical energy and stored in glucose molecules.

In the presence of **chlorophyll**, light provides the energy for carbon dioxide and water to undergo a series of **enzyme-controlled reactions** to make glucose and oxygen. The glucose is often rapidly changed into starch. The oxygen is used by organisms for respiration.

> **Photosynthesis can be summarised as:**
> **carbon dioxide ✛ water ✛ light energy → glucose ✛ oxygen**

The main factors which limit the rate of photosynthesis are the availability of carbon dioxide, light, and chlorophyll. As enzymes are involved, temperature can also be a limiting factor.

Photosynthesis has two basic stages:

Stage one

Energy from sunlight is trapped by chlorophyll and splits molecules of water into hydrogen and oxygen.

Stage two

Hydrogen combines with carbon dioxide in a complex series of reactions which are the starting points for the manufacture of all carbohydrates, fats, proteins and some vitamins.

Photosynthesis provides food and oxygen for animals. It also uses carbon dioxide from respiration to maintain a constant level of carbon dioxide in the atmosphere.

Test yourself

1 To test a leaf for starch it is first decolourised by being boiled in alcohol, washed in water and having a chemical added.
   a) What is the chemical?
   b) How will its colour change if starch is present?

2 List two advantages of having plants in an aquarium tank containing fish.

3 Give a definition of photosynthesis.

4 Two specimen tubes were set up as shown in the diagram:

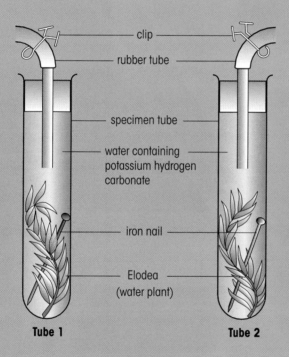

The water in the tubes was boiled to remove air before the plants were added. Tube 1 was left in the dark and tube 2 was left in the light. After 48 hours the nail in tube 2 was rusty, but the nail in tube 1 was not. Explain why the process taking place in the plant in tube 2 caused the nail to go rusty.

Green plants as organisms

BBC GCSE Check and Test: Science

Check the facts

The process by which water is lost from plants is called transpiration.

Water evaporating from the leaves of a plant pulls up more water containing dissolved minerals from the soil.

Much of the water is lost through tiny pores, called **stomata**, which occur on the surface of the leaves.

Transpiration also helps to cool leaves by **evaporation**.

The column of water is carried through the narrow xylem vessels which extend from the root through the stem to the leaves.

The column is prevented from breaking up by strong attractive forces between the water molecules. This is called **cohesion**.

Test yourself

1 Name the structures in the leaf through which water is lost.

2 Name the process by which water is normally lost through the leaf.

3 An experiment to show water loss was carried out with three leaves of the same size. A waterproof layer of grease was put on the leaves as shown below:

Leaf A	upper surface only
Leaf B	lower surface only
Leaf C	both surfaces.

The leaves were weighed and then hung in a warm room for eight hours. The results are shown in the table below:

Leaf	Mass at beginning (g)	Mass after 8 hours (g)
A	6	3
B	6	5.5
C	7	7

a) What was the loss in mass from each of the three leaves?

b) Through which surface did the greatest water loss occur?

Check the facts

Growth in plants is regulated by hormones. These are made in certain parts of the plant and are carried to other parts.

> **Hormones influence growth, division, and elongation of cells.**

The most widely-studied plant hormones are called **auxins**. Different parts of the plant react differently to auxins.

A high concentration of auxin seems to stimulate stem growth but inhibit the growth of roots.

Auxins control growth movements in response to a directional stimulus, such as light from one side. The auxin builds up on the dark side of a stem, causing it to bend towards the light. This is called **phototropism**.

Example

Auxins can be used in selective weedkillers where broad-leaved weeds such as dandelions are killed by high concentrations, but grass is unharmed.

 Test yourself

The following apparatus was used to investigate the effect of a one-sided stimulus of light on the direction of growth in plant stems.

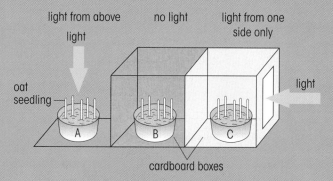

light from above   no light   light from one side only

light

oat seedling

light

A   B   C

cardboard boxes

1 The plants were left as shown for three days and then the seedlings were examined. Describe the expected appearance of the seedlings in A, B and C after three days.

2 Name one other directional stimulus that affects growth movements in plants and describe its effects on roots and stems.

3 What type of chemical is responsible for the growth responses in plants?

4 Why is phototropism beneficial to the plant?

Green plants as organisms

BBC GCSE Check and Test: Science

Variation, inheritance and evolution

 Check the facts

> **Natural selection is an evolutionary mechanism by which the total environment selects those forms that are best-suited to breed.**

Charles Darwin's theory of natural selection is based on three observations and two deductions:

ⓗ

Observation 1	Organisms are capable of reproducing in geometric progression, that is: 2, 4, 8, 16 and so on.
Observation 2	Numbers of a species tend to remain constant over long periods of time.
Deduction 1	Most offspring do not survive to breed.
Observation 3	All living things show variation.
Deduction 2	By natural selection, those best adapted to their environment are more likely to survive to reproduce and pass on their **genes**. This is known as 'survival of the fittest', since they 'fit' their environment.

Test yourself

1 Which of the following statements is **not** involved in natural selection?
 a) Choice of a suitable habitat. b) Human selection of the best species.
 c) Survival of the strongest.   d) Survival of the fittest to breed.

There are light- and dark-coloured Peppered moths. Both are eaten by birds. Before the Clean Air Act (1956), both types of moth were released in two different areas and as many as possible were recaptured. One group was released near an industrial area where soot covered the trees. The other was released in a non-industrial area. The percentages of moths recaptured in the two areas are shown below.

ⓗ

Area	Percentage recaptured	
	Light-coloured type	Dark-coloured type
Non-industrial	12.5	6.3
Industrial	13.1	27.5

2 How do these data support the theory of natural selection?

Check the facts

> **Mutations are sudden genetic changes. There are two types:**
> • gene mutation   • **chromosome mutation**

Gene mutation

Gene mutation (point mutation) arises when part of the genetic code in a **DNA** molecule is accidentally altered when the DNA is copied. Such changes alter or destroy a characteristic controlled by one or more genes.

Chromosome mutation

This is less common than gene mutation. It may result in abnormal chromosome numbers when cells divide to form eggs or sperm.

The frequency of mutations is increased by factors called **mutagens**. These include certain chemicals and radiation from radioactive elements.

Test yourself

1 Which of the following statements is **untrue**?
 a) All mutations are harmful.
 b) Mutation can be caused by atomic radiation.
 c) Mutation can be caused by certain chemicals.
 d) Mutations can be inherited.

2 In the 1950s there was widespread testing of nuclear weapons on islands in the Pacific Ocean. On one such island, before nuclear testing, there was much grass which was food for two forms of a species of snail. One form was striped yellow and black. The other was a rarer black form. Birds were the main predators of the snails.

Why do you think the black form was rarer?

3 The testing of nuclear weapons destroys vegetation and blackens rocks. What effect would you expect this to have on the numbers of the black form of the snail?

4 Many years after the testing of nuclear weapons on the island had finished, scientists visited the island and discovered a new brown form of the species. How might this have arisen?

Variation, inheritance and evolution

BBC GCSE Check and Test: Science

Check the facts

In mammals there are two types of chromosome:
- **the X chromosome**
- **the Y chromosome**

The chromosomes that determine gender are called **sex chromosomes**.

h In human males they can be distinguished from the other chromosomes as the Y chromosome is shorter than the X chromosome it is paired with.

Males	1 X and 1 Y chromosome
Females	2 X chromosomes

Humans have 22 pairs of ordinary chromosomes and 1 pair of sex chromosomes. Some genes occur only on the X chromosomes and they are said to be sex-linked.

Test yourself

1 This diagram represents part of a living cell.

Name the structures labelled A and B.

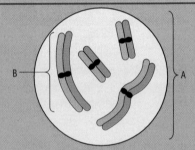

2 a) Copy the diagram below and write the correct sex chromosomes in the fertilised eggs, A and B.

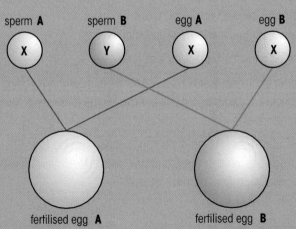

b) State the gender of each of the fertilised eggs, A and B.

Check the facts

Alleles are alternative forms of a gene for a particular characteristic.

> **The outward appearance of an organism is its phenotype
> and its genetic makeup is its genotype.**

Steps in solving genetics problems

- Assign a symbol for each allele, usually a capital letter for a dominant allele and a lower case letter for a recessive allele.
  For example, T = allele for tallness, t = allele for shortness.

- Determine the genotype of each parent and indicate a mating.
  For example, Tt x tt.

- Determine all the possible types of sex cells each parent can produce.
  In this example, Tt → T and t, tt → t and t.

- Determine all the allele combinations that can result when the sex cells unite by drawing a diagram.
  In this example the possible allele combinations are Tt, Tt, tt and tt:

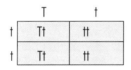

	T	t
t	Tt	tt
t	Tt	tt

- Determine the phenotypes. In this example, two tall and two short.

Test yourself

1 In koala bears, brown or white hair is controlled by a pair of alleles. Allele B (for brown hair) is dominant to allele b (for white hair). Name the structure in the nucleus of a cell where you would find the alleles.

2 a) What is the genotype of a white koala bear?

b) State the two possible genotypes of a brown koala bear.

3 A zoo keeper had a pair of brown koala bears. These were mated together and the offspring was white.

a) What were the genotypes of the parents?

b) What would be the chances of producing a white koala bear from a mating between a white koala and one of the parents in part a)?

Variation, inheritance and evolution

BBC GCSE Check and Test: Science

Variation, inheritance and evolution

Check the facts

> **Gene mutations may lead to inherited genetic abnormalities – at least 4000 abnormalities like this are known in humans.**

The most common human inherited disease is **cystic fibrosis**. This is inherited as a recessive allele and causes the respiratory bronchioles, and the tubes leading from the pancreas and liver to be blocked by mucus. Disease-causing bacteria can become trapped in the mucus in the lungs.

(h) **Huntington's disease** is caused by inheriting a dominant allele, which doesn't manifest until aged 30–40. It causes deterioration of the nervous system.

Haemophilia is characterised by blood that doesn't clot. Women can carry the disease allele harmlessly as it is sex-linked and recessive. The gene is on the X chromosome at a position that doesn't pair with the Y chromosome. In a female if the dominant allele for normal blood clotting is carried on one X chromosome and the recessive allele for haemophilia is on the other she will not develop the disease. The male only has one X chromosome, so if it carries the recessive allele, he will suffer from the condition.

Test yourself

1 What is meant by the term 'inherited disease'?

2 Explain why sufferers of cystic fibrosis find breathing difficult.

3 Suggest why antibiotics help people who suffer from cystic fibrosis.

4 Tracy and Peter do not suffer from cystic fibrosis but one of their children, David, does suffer from it. The family pedigree is shown in this diagram.

(h)

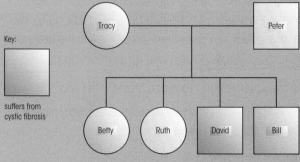

Key:

suffers from cystic fibrosis

Tracy — Peter

Betty   Ruth   David   Bill

Use these letters in your answers:
N = normal (dominant) and n = cystic fibrosis (recessive).

a) What is the genotype of i) Tracy   ii) Peter   iii) David?

b) What are the two possibilities of Gwyn's genotype?

Check the facts

> **Genes are made of a chemical called deoxyribonucleic acid (DNA) which controls all living processes.**

DNA consists of a **double helix**, a ladder-like structure twisted into a spiral. The 'sides' of the ladder are each made up of alternating phosphate and deoxyribose sugar units.

The 'rungs' are composed of pairs of **bases**. Each base is joined to its partner by weak bonds. The partner bases are adenine (A) with thymine (T) and cytosine (C) with guanine (G). The order of the bases forms a 'code' for the production of proteins.

Each gene is made of a DNA molecule with a characteristic arrangement of bases. A change of just one base can sometimes alter a particular gene.

There is an almost unlimited number of possible arrangements if you consider that a strand of DNA can be over 10 000 base units long. So there is an almost unlimited number of possible genes in all plants and animals.

Test yourself

1 a) What is the name given to the shape of the DNA molecule?

b) This diagram shows part of a molecule of DNA. Using the same letters as in the diagram, give letters for the missing bases.

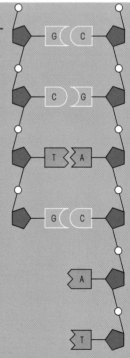

2 Genes are made of DNA which controls the production of proteins. One group of proteins in cells controls reactions by acting as catalysts. What are these proteins called?

Variation, inheritance and evolution

BBC GCSE Check and Test: Science

Check the facts

The most common type of genetic engineering uses enzymes to isolate a gene from one organism and put it into another.

(h) Scientists have isolated human genes that make **hormones** (**blood proteins**). They insert the genes into bacteria or yeasts and these **microbes** make identical copies of themselves by **cloning**. Because the microbe now contains the human gene, it can make the human hormone. The process is rapid and relatively cheap so large quantities of valuable hormones can be harvested and used to treat various disorders.

Test yourself

1 Insulin is a hormone used to control diabetes, which can be extracted from the pancreas of pigs and cattle. Human insulin is now produced by genetic engineering. The diagram shows the first stages of this process:

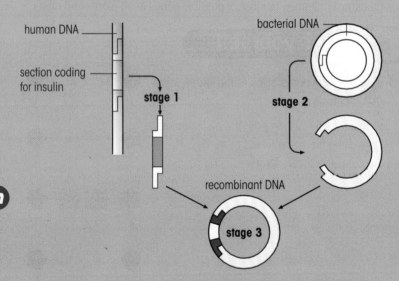

State what is happening at each of the labelled stages by matching the correct statement to the number of the stage.

a) The DNA of the bacterium is cut.

b) A gene is removed from a human cell.

c) A human gene is inserted into the DNA of the bacterium.

2 Name the types of chemical needed at stages 1 and 2.

3 When bacteria have the recombinant DNA, as in stage 3, they undergo the process of cloning. What is meant by 'cloning'?

Check the facts

Green plants convert energy from the Sun's radiation into stored chemical energy.

Much of this stored energy is released when plants are eaten.

Some of it is stored in the bodies of **herbivores**.

When a **carnivore** feeds on a herbivore, some energy is used and some is stored in the carnivore.

> **A food chain traces the direction of energy flow through the various types of feeders, that is:**
> **producer → herbivore → carnivore**

Test yourself

Some of the animals which live in or near an oak tree

Animal	Food
bark beetle	bark
blackbird	earthworms, beetles, caterpillars
caterpillar	leaves
earthworm	dead leaves
hawk	small birds
mouse	acorns
owl	mice
squirrel	acorns

1 From the data, name:

a) the producer
b) a herbivore
c) a carnivore.

2 Make a food chain with three links beginning with bark.

3 Explain the possible effect of a reduction in the owl population on:

a) mice
b) squirrels.

Living things in their environment

Check the facts

> One dangerous form of water **pollution** is caused by industrial wastes containing heavy metals, such as mercury, lead, zinc and cadmium.

These heavy metals are by-products of mining and manufacturing processes. The concentration of heavy metals increases through food chains until those animals at the top of the chains are poisoned.

Heavy metals interfere with the actions of many vital **enzymes** in animals and so cause death.

Some insecticides, such as DDT, also increase in concentration from a harmless level at the beginning of the chain to toxic levels in top carnivores.

Test yourself

Look at the cartoon

Have you been spraying your roses again?

Assume that the food chain in the pond is:

algae → small animals → larger animals → fish

1 Roses close to the pond were sprayed with an insecticide. Explain how this affected the fish in the pond.

www.bbc.co.uk/revision

Check the facts

Inter-linked food chains are called food webs.

Food webs give a more accurate picture of the feeding relationships within communities than food chains.

Example

In an oak tree, there will be hundreds of different species which act as food, feeders or both.

Even the most complex diagram of a food web will not be entirely accurate because many species eat almost any available food and some change their feeding habits during the course of their lives.

Example

A caterpillar may feed exclusively on leaves, but after it has changed into a butterfly, it becomes a nectar feeder.

Test yourself

The diagram shows a food web in a forest

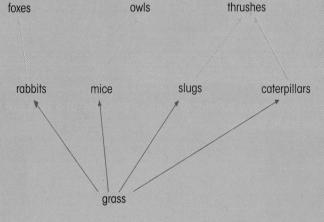

1 Why do all food chains begin with plants?

2 What is represented by the arrows?

3 If all the rabbits were killed by a disease, what two effects would this have upon other animals in the food web?

Living things in their environment

Check the facts

Food pyramids show how much energy is available to organisms living in a measured area of land or a measured volume of water.

There are three ways to represent these pyramids:

1
A pyramid of numbers, which shows the number of organisms per unit area or volume in each feeding (trophic) level.

2
A pyramid of biomass, which shows the mass of organic material per unit area or volume in each trophic level.

3
A pyramid of energy, which shows the energy content at each trophic level, and the energy losses at each level.

Test yourself

The biomass and names of some organisms in a lake are shown in the table below:

Organism	Biomass (kg)
insects and leeches	500
large fish	5
plants	50 000
small fish	50
snails and worms	5000

1 Draw a pyramid of biomass using the information given in the table.

2 Which of the organisms are likely to be present in the least numbers?

Check the facts

> As a result of the carbon cycle, the concentration of carbon dioxide in the atmosphere should remain constant and there should be enough for plants to carry out photosynthesis.

During **respiration**, glucose (which contains carbon) is oxidised, releasing carbon dioxide into the environment. If there were no process to balance the effects of respiration, the carbon dioxide level in the atmosphere would increase and we would eventually run out of oxygen.

When plants photosynthesise, they take in the carbon dioxide that would otherwise accumulate.

The food made by plants enters food chains, but eventually plants and animals die. The bacteria involved in decomposition return carbon dioxide to the atmosphere by their respiration.

Test yourself

The diagram shows the circulation of carbon in nature

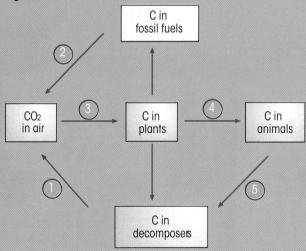

1 Match pathways 1 to 5 with the processes listed below.

> burning of coal and oil
> feeding
> photosynthesis
> respiration by microbes
> decay

Living things in their environment

BBC GCSE Check and Test: Science

Living things in their environment

Check the facts

The nitrogen cycle helps to maintain a constant amount of nitrate in the soil.

The nitrogen cycle relies on two groups of microbes:

1 Those that break down large molecules containing nitrogen into smaller molecules.

2 Those that build up small molecules containing nitrogen into larger molecules.

h

The microbes which break down large molecules are:

• putrefying bacteria and fungi

• denitrifying bacteria which break down nitrates into nitrogen.

The microbes which build up larger molecules are:

• nitrifying bacteria which make nitrates out of ammonium compounds

• nitrogen-fixing bacteria which change nitrogen into compounds that can be absorbed by plants.

Test yourself

The diagram shows part of the nitrogen cycle

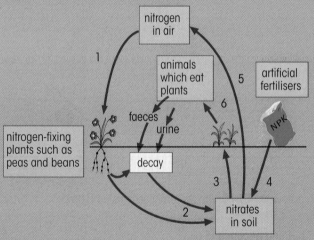

h

www.bbc.co.uk/revision

1 In what form do animals take in nitrogen by feeding?

2 State two types of microbe which are responsible for decay.

3 Which three numbers on the diagram represent places where microbes are involved in the nitrogen cycle?

Check the facts

Atoms consist of electrons circulating around a heavy nucleus of protons and neutrons.

These sub-atomic particles have mass and electrical charge.

Name	Symbol	Relative mass	Relative charge
proton	p	1	+1
neutron	n	1	0
electron	e	$\frac{1}{1840}$ (negligible)	−1

The attraction between positive and negative holds the electrons around the nucleus. Atoms are neutral because the number of protons is equal to the number of electrons. The number of protons is the **atomic number** (**Z**).

Total number of protons + neutrons = mass number (A)

Atoms of an **element** always have the same number of protons (atomic number), but can have different numbers of neutrons (mass numbers). These are known as **isotopes**.

Test yourself

1 Fill in the numbers missing from the table

Atom	Sodium	Aluminium	Fluorine
number of protons	11		9
number of neutrons	12		
number of electrons			
atomic number		13	
mass number		27	17

2 How many protons, neutrons and electrons does each of these contain:

a) $^{14}_{7}N$ b) $^{11}_{5}B$ c) $^{127}_{53}I$ d) $^{31}_{15}P$ e) $^{56}_{26}N$?

3 Explain why all atoms are electrically neutral.

4 Explain why the particles orbiting the nucleus do not fly away from it.

5 Oxygen has three isotopes: $^{16}_{8}O$, $^{17}_{8}O$ and $^{18}_{8}O$.

Explain the similarities and differences between them.

Elements and compounds

BBC GCSE Check and Test: Science

Elements and compounds

Check the facts

Electrons orbit the nucleus in a series of **shells** or energy levels. Each energy level has a maximum number of electrons it can contain.

First shell	holds up to two electrons – this is the lowest energy level
Second shell	holds up to eight electrons
Third shell	has two sub-levels: the first holds eight electrons and the second ten; eighteen in total
Fourth shell	has three sub-levels: the first holds eight electrons, the second ten and the third fourteen (32 in total)

Energy levels are filled with electrons in order from the lowest energy level.

The final arrangement of electrons is the electronic configuration of the atom.

Example

$^{24}_{12}$Mg has twelve protons and thus twelve electrons. The electronic configuration will be 2.8.2, as shown in the diagram.

Test yourself

1 What is meant by 'electronic configuration'?

2 What is the electronic configuration of:

a) $_6$C b) $_8$O c) $_{17}$Cl d) $_{18}$Ar?

3 $^{23}_{11}$Na is a sodium atom. For this atom state:

a) the atomic number
b) the mass number
c) the number of electrons
d) the number of neutrons
e) the electronic configuration.

4 Draw a sketch showing the complete atomic structure of $^{27}_{13}$Al.

5 What do $^{14}_7$N and $^{31}_{15}$P have in common?

6 The first two electrons in level 4 have a lower energy level than the second sub-level (of ten electrons) in level 3. What is the electronic configuration of:

a) $_{19}$K b) $_{20}$Ca c) $_{21}$Sc

Check the facts

Carbon atoms have four electrons in their outer shell, so they can form **covalent bonds** with four other atoms.

Example

methane, CH_4

Carbon atoms are the only atoms that can make different length chains. There are an infinite number of possible carbon compounds.

$-\overset{|}{\underset{|}{C}}-\overset{|}{\underset{|}{C}}-\overset{|}{\underset{|}{C}}-\overset{|}{\underset{|}{C}}-\overset{|}{\underset{|}{C}}-\overset{|}{\underset{|}{C}}-$

The study of carbon compounds is a branch of chemistry in itself. It is called organic chemistry.

The simplest carbon compounds, called **hydrocarbons**, contain hydrogen and carbon. The simplest hydrocarbons are **alkanes**, containing only single bonds. Compounds containing only single bonds are **saturated compounds**.

Another group of hydrocarbons is the **alkenes**. They contain at least one pair of carbon atoms joined by two shared pairs of electrons, i.e. double bonds. Compounds containing double bonds are **unsaturated compounds**.

Some organic compounds, called **non-hydrocarbons** contain other elements.

Examples

alcohols	contain the —OH group, e.g. C_2H_5OH (ethanol)
acids	contain the —COOH group, e.g. $CH_3.COOH$ (ethanoic acid)
chlorides	contain —Cl, e.g. C_2H_5Cl (chloroethane)
amines	contain the —NH_2 group, e.g. $C_2H_5NH_2$ (ethylamine)

Test yourself

1 What is organic chemistry?

2 What is a hydrocarbon?

3 What property of carbon allows it to form more compounds than all the other elements put together?

4 a) What is a saturated compound?
b) What is an unsaturated compound?

5 Suggest the molecular formula of:
a) methanol   b) chloropropane   c) methylamine.

Elements and compounds

BBC GCSE Check and Test: Science

Check the facts

When two non-metal atoms react together, both need to gain electrons. They achieve this by sharing their outer electrons.

Atoms are joined by shared pairs of electrons. One electron from each atom makes up the pair.

The atoms are joined because the shared pair of electrons circulates around each of them. This is a covalent bond.

Example

The formation of methane (CH_4) from carbon and hydrogen.

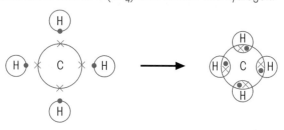

Each carbon atom has four outer electrons. Each hydrogen atom has one outer electron. Sharing gives both of them full **shells**.

The atoms are bonded together into a molecule, which is separate from other molecules.

Forces between molecules are low and are easily overcome so the molecules are free to move around randomly.

Compounds with covalent molecules have low melting and boiling points and do not conduct electricity.

Sometimes covalent bonding produces **giant structures** by bonding atoms.

These giant structures are hard solids with very high melting points.

Examples	
Diamond	carbon atoms covalently bonded into a continuous giant structure
Sand	silicon and oxygen atoms in a covalent giant structure

Sometimes atoms are joined by two shared pairs of electrons and this is called a **double bond**. An example of this is the oxygen molecule, O_2:

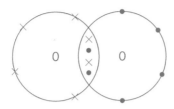

h In the nitrogen molecule, N_2, the bond is a triple bond.

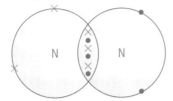

This double- or triple-bond formation is necessary to complete the outer shells of each atom.

Test yourself

1 What is a covalent bond?

2 What is a molecule?

3 Why do covalent compounds with simple molecules have low melting and boiling points?

4 Draw dot and cross diagrams to show the bonding in:
   a) water (H_2O)   b) ammonia (NH_3)   c) chlorine (Cl_2).

5 Why do giant structures have high melting points?

h **6** What is a double bond?

7 The compound ethene, C_2H_4, has a double bond between the two carbon atoms and single bonds between the carbon and hydrogen atoms as shown below.

$$\begin{array}{ccc} H & & H \\ \diagdown & & \diagup \\ & C=C & \\ \diagup & & \diagdown \\ H & & H \end{array}$$

Draw a dot and cross diagram to show the bonding in ethene.

Elements and compounds

BBC GCSE Check and Test: Science

Check the facts

The way that **elements** react depends upon the arrangement of electrons in their atoms.

Only the electrons in the **outer shell** are involved. The nucleus and inner electrons do not change.

> **Metal ions are positive; non-metal ions are negative.**

Atoms react to achieve a complete outer electron shell.

All **compounds** involving metals are formed by ionic bonds.

The metal atom loses its outermost electrons. It is now a **positive ion** because it has more protons than electrons.

The non-metal atom gains these electrons into its outermost shell. It is now a negative ion because it has more electrons than protons.

> **The attraction between these oppositely-charged ions is the bond that holds them together. It is called an ionic bond.**

Example

The formation of sodium chloride from sodium and chlorine.

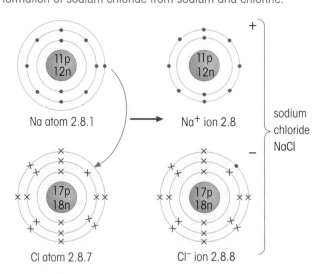

Na atom 2.8.1   Na$^+$ ion 2.8

Cl atom 2.8.7   Cl$^-$ ion 2.8.8

sodium chloride NaCl

The number of positive or negative charges on an ion equals the number of electrons lost or gained.

A sodium chloride crystal is a **giant lattice** made up of unipositive (one plus charge) Na$^+$ ions held to uninegative Cl$^-$ ions by the attraction of positive for negative.

All ionic compounds are giant lattices of this type. They are solids with a high melting point. They conduct electricity when melted or in solution in water.

Some compounds are formed by the transfer of more than one electron. These compounds contain multi-charged ions.

> **Example**
>
> The formation of magnesium oxide.
>
> 2+
>
> 12p
> 12n
>
> 12p
> 12n
>
> Mg atom 2.8.2   → Mg^{2+} ion 2.8
>
> magnesium oxide MgO
>
> 8p
> 8n
>
> 8p
> 8n
>
> 2–
>
> O atom 2.6 O^{2-} ion 2.8

Test yourself

1 What is an ion?

2 What is a unipositive ion?

You will need a periodic table for questions 3 and 4 (**see topic 52**).

3 The sodium ion has the symbol Na^+. What is the symbol of the ions of:
a) potassium   b) calcium
c) oxygen   d) magnesium
e) bromine?

4 Draw dot and cross diagrams to explain the formation of:
a) lithium fluoride
b) calcium oxide

5 State one similarity and one difference between:
a) the magnesium ion and the sodium ion
b) the magnesium ion and the oxide ion.

BBC GCSE Check and Test: Science

Check the facts

Extraction of materials

> **The reactivity series is a list of metals arranged in order of reactivity, the most reactive at the top.**

Reactive metals are difficult to extract from ores whilst less reactive metals are extracted more easily.

	Metal	Extraction	
most reactive	potassium sodium calcium magnesium aluminium	by electrolysis (topic 42)	**most difficult to extract**
	zinc iron lead copper mercury	by reduction of the oxide (topic 41)	**easiest to extract**
least reactive	silver gold	found naturally	

Metals can be displaced from compounds by more reactive metals, e.g:

$$Zn\ (s) + CuSO_4\ (aq) \rightarrow ZnSO_4\ (aq) + Cu\ (s)$$

$$Al\ (s) + Na_2SO_4\ (aq) \rightarrow no\ reaction$$

Test yourself

1 What is the 'reactivity series'?

2 Name two metals more reactive than aluminium and two metals less reactive than iron.

3 For each of the following pairs write a word equation if you predict they will react and 'no reaction' if you predict otherwise:
a) zinc and lead nitrate   b) lead and copper sulphate
c) zinc and magnesium chloride   d) copper and silver nitrate.

4 Electrolysis is used to extract lithium from its ore. What does this tell you about lithium?

5 Explain why reactive metals are difficult to extract.

Check the facts

The rocks in the Earth's crust are mixtures of minerals. From these rocks we make many materials (e.g. glass, building materials, ceramics, acids, alkalis, hydrogen, chlorine). Some rocks are composed mainly of the compounds of one metal, so it is possible to obtain pure samples of the metal.

Rocks from which we extract metals are called ores.

Less reactive metals (zinc to copper) are obtained by **reducing the oxide,**

For more on reduction, see topic 61.

Examples

1 The main zinc ore is zinc blende (mostly zinc sulphide). It is roasted in air, converting it to oxide, which reduces to zinc by roasting with coke (carbon).

$$2ZnS\ (s) + 3O_2\ (g) \rightarrow 2ZnO\ (s) + 2SO_2\ (g)$$
$$2ZnO\ (s) + C\ (s) \rightarrow 2Zn\ (s) + CO_2\ (g)$$

2 The main ore of iron is haematite (mainly iron (III) oxide). It is reduced to iron by carbon monoxide in a blast furnace.

$$Fe_2O_3\ (s) + 3CO\ (g) \rightarrow 2Fe\ (s) + 3CO_2\ (g)$$

3 Metals such as mercury are so unreactive that their compounds split up on heating to leave the metal. This is called thermal decomposition.

$$2HgO\ (s) \rightarrow 2Hg\ (l) + O_2\ (g)$$

For more on thermal decomposition, see topic 63.

Test yourself

1 What is the definition of an ore?

2 Name four metals obtained from their ores by reduction of the oxide.

3 Name the main ore of zinc. Outline the extraction of zinc from this ore.

4 Lead can be obtained from lead oxide by heating the lead oxide on a carbon block. Write a balanced chemical equation for this reaction and name all the materials.

Extraction of materials

BBC GCSE Check and Test: Science

Extraction of materials

Check the facts

Sodium from sodium chloride

Solid sodium chloride is made up of Na^+ and Cl^- ions held in a rigid lattice.

For more on lattices, see topic 39.

Because the **ions** cannot move, solid sodium chloride cannot conduct electricity.

When sodium chloride is melted, the lattice breaks down and the ions are free to move. As a result, molten sodium chloride can conduct electricity.

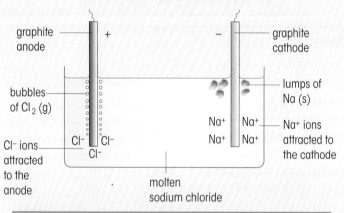

h

Ions present:	$NaCl \longrightarrow Na^+ + Cl^-$
At anode (+):	Cl^- ions are attracted and lose electrons.
	$2Cl^- - 2e^- \longrightarrow Cl_2 \ (g)$
At cathode (−):	Na^+ ions are attracted and gain electrons.
	$2Na^+ + 2e^- \longrightarrow 2Na \ (s)$
Overall:	$2NaCl \ (l) \longrightarrow 2Na \ (s) + Cl_2 \ (g)$

Purification of copper

Copper is extracted from its ore, copper pyrites (mainly copper I sulphide, Cu_2S), by heating the ore in air. This reduces it to copper.

$$Cu_2S \ (s) + O_2 \ (g) \rightarrow 2Cu \ (s) + SO_2 \ (g)$$

The copper is 98% pure and is called blister copper.

Blister copper is purified by making it the anode of an electrolytic cell in which the cathode is pure copper and the **electrolyte** is an aqueous solution of copper sulphate.

www.bbc.co.uk/revision

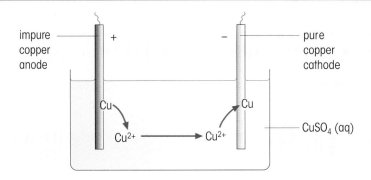

Ions present: $CuSO_4 \longrightarrow Cu^{2+} + SO_4^{2-}$

At anode (+): The Cu atoms of the anode each give up two electrons.

$Cu\ (s) \longrightarrow Cu^{2+}\ (aq) + 2e^-$

At cathode (−): The $Cu^{2+}\ (aq)$ ions are attracted and each gain two electrons.

$Cu^{2+}\ (aq) + 2e^- \longrightarrow Cu\ (s)$

Overall: Electrolysis results in the copper dissolving from the anode and pure copper being deposited onto the cathode.

Test yourself

1 Why does molten sodium chloride conduct electricity when solid sodium chloride is a non-conductor?

2 Give the name and symbol of each ion in sodium chloride.

3 With equations, explain what happens when molten NaCl is electrolysed.

4 What is blister copper? Outline how it is obtained from copper pyrites.

5 Using the examples above to help, explain fully, with equations, what happens when the following are electrolysed:

a) molten potassium chloride (KCl)   b) molten aluminium oxide (Al_2O_3).

6 Sodium chloride melts at 800°C when the rigid lattice of Na^+ and Cl^- ions breaks down. Aluminium oxide melts at 2400°C. Suggest a possible explanation for the melting point of Al_2O_3 being three times that of NaCl.

Organic chemistry

Check the facts

Crude oil is a **fossil fuel** formed over millions of years from plant and animal remains. It is a mixture of **hydrocarbons** with chains from one to hundreds of carbon atoms.

These compounds have different boiling points and so can be separated by fractional distillation.

Temperature	Name of fraction	No. of C atoms in chain	Uses
about room temperature	gas	1–4	separated into simple alkanes and used as fuels
70°C	petrol	5–10	vehicle fuel
	paraffins	10–16	aviation fuel, heating fuel, manufacture of detergents
240°C	diesel	16–20	diesel fuel, manufacture of various chemicals
350°C	lubricating oils and waxes	20–60	fuels for power stations, ships, manufacture of waxes and greases
400–500°C	bitumen	60 plus	roads, roofing, waterproofing

Most of the products are used for fuel as hydrocarbons burn easily in air.

Example

$$C_3H_8 \text{ (g)} + 5O_2 \text{ (g)} \rightarrow 3CO_2 \text{ (g)} + 4H_2O \text{ (g)} + heat$$

propane

Test yourself

1 Why is crude oil described as a fossil fuel?

2 What is fractional distillation?

3 For three of the fractions obtained from crude oil, state the approximate temperature at which each boils off, the approximate length of its carbon chains and its uses.

4 Write a balanced chemical equation for the burning in air of:
   a) methane CH_4 b) butane C_4H_{10} (c) decane $C_{10}H_{22}$.

Check the facts

There is greater demand for short chain fractions of crude oil (such as petrol) than long chain ones (such as diesel). Heating long hydrocarbon molecules to high temperatures, usually with a catalyst, breaks them down into smaller molecules. This is called **cracking**.

Example

$$C_{19}H_{40} \xrightarrow[\text{catalyst}]{\text{heat}} C_{10}H_{22} + C_4H_8 + C_3H_6 + C_2H_4$$

Cracking also produces unsaturated hydrocarbons called **alkenes**, which undergo polymerisation.

For more on alkenes, see topic 37.

Double-bonded ethene molecules will, if heated under pressure with a catalyst, join to form long chains of carbon atoms.

The giant molecule produced is polythene (a **polymer**). The individual ethene molecules are monomers.

Making polymers from monomers is called polymerisation.

Polythene, made by adding monomers together, is an **addition polymer**.

Test yourself

1 What is cracking?

2 Why can alkenes undergo polymerisation?

3 Explain polymerisation, giving an example.

Include an explanation of 'monomer' in your answer.

4 The structural formula of vinyl chloride is

Draw the structural formula of a section of a molecule of the polymer polyvinyl chloride (PVC).

Organic chemistry

BBC GCSE Check and Test: Science

Check the facts

Earth and air

> **Air is made up of:**
> • 78% nitrogen • 21% oxygen • 1% other gases
> (the most important one is carbon dioxide)

Nitrogen from air is used to make ammonia, which is required in the manufacture of fertilisers for agriculture.

The Haber process

Nitrogen from air is combined with hydrogen (obtained from methane, CH_4) to produce ammonia.

$$N_2 \text{ (g)} + 3H_2 \text{ (g)} \underset{\substack{500-550°C \\ \text{Fe catalyst}}}{\overset{250 \text{ atmospheres}}{\rightleftharpoons}} 2NH_3 \text{ (g)} + \text{heat}$$

> For more on the Haber process, see topic 68.

Manufacture of fertilisers

The two most important nitrogenous fertilisers (nitrogen-containing fertilisers) are ammonium sulphate and ammonium nitrate. They are manufactured by reacting ammonia with dilute sulphuric acid or dilute nitric acid.

$$2NH_3 \text{ (g)} + H_2SO_4 \text{ (aq)} \rightarrow (NH_4)_2SO_4 \text{ (aq)}$$

$$NH_3 \text{ (g)} + HNO_3 \text{ (aq)} \rightarrow NH_4NO_3 \text{ (aq)}$$

Fertilisers and plants

- Nitrogen is an essential constituent of living matter. Nitrogen compounds, particularly proteins, are needed for healthy growth.
- Plants make **proteins** by taking nitrogen compounds from the soil and converting them to protein.
- Using the same soil continuously eventually uses up nutrients. They are replaced by adding fertilisers.
- Fertilisers produce high yields of healthy crops quickly.

Fertilisers and pollution

- Rain washes fertilisers into rivers and lakes. The fertilisers cause algae and bacteria to grow. These use oxygen and reduce light levels causing fish and plants to die.
- Rain washes fertilisers into reservoirs and hence into drinking water. It is thought that nitrates may affect the health of babies and old people.

Test yourself

1. Name the three main gases present in air.

2. State the percentages of the two most common gases in air.

3. What is manufactured in the Haber process?

4. Where does the nitrogen come from that is used in the Haber process?

5. State the conditions and write a balanced equation for the Haber process.

6. What is a 'nitrogenous' fertiliser?

7. Write balanced equations for the conversion of ammonia into two nitrogenous fertilisers.

8. Why do plants need nitrogen?

9. How do plants make the protein they need?

10. Why do farmers need to use fertilisers?

11. What effect do fertilisers have on crops?

Earth and air

Check the facts

Earth and air

The table below indicates how the atmosphere may have evolved.

Number of years ago/process	Effect
4500 million • Earth forms • volcanoes begin to erupt	• atmosphere probably mainly hydrogen and helium • methane, carbon dioxide and water vapour are added to the atmosphere • the very light hydrogen and helium begin to drift off into space
3800 million • solid rocks form • water vapour condenses	• seas form • pure water at first but over time minerals from the Earth's crust dissolve in them
3500 million • first simple plant life appears	• plants begin to photosynthesise, taking CO_2 from the atmosphere and releasing oxygen • some of this oxygen dissolves in the sea
2500 → 400 million • animal life begins on land and atmosphere becomes as it is today	• animals use oxygen for respiration and so plants and animals begin to maintain a balance of carbon dioxide and oxygen in the atmosphere
present (and future?) • burning fossil fuels and clearing forests	• burning fossil fuels produces CO_2 • cutting down trees removes plants which use up CO_2 • hence the CO_2/O_2 balance is changing, with CO_2 increasing • this heavy gas remains in the atmosphere and traps heat (greenhouse effect)

Test yourself

1 Explain how oxygen was added to the atmosphere.

2 Explain how the level of oxygen might have changed over time and why it is now quite stable.

3 Outline how the seas may have evolved from reasonably pure condensed water vapour to their present state.

4 How does clearing forests add to the greenhouse effect?

Check the facts

Materials on Earth and in the atmosphere are undergoing constant change, but a balance must always be maintained.

> **Nature achieves balance by recycling material.**
> **The most important natural cycles are the nitrogen and carbon cycles and the water and oxygen cycles.**

The carbon cycle keeps the **carbon dioxide** level in the atmosphere in balance. Carbon leaves the atmosphere by one route only: carbon dioxide being absorbed into plants by **photosynthesis.**

Carbon returns to the atmosphere by three routes:

1 plants and animals releasing CO_2 during **respiration**

2 **bacteria** feeding on dead plants and animals and releasing CO_2

3 dead plants and animals form **fossil fuels** which release CO_2 on burning.

The balance could be easily disturbed if there were fewer plants or more fuel was burnt.

> **For more on the atmosphere, see topic 46.**

The diagram below summarises the carbon cycle.

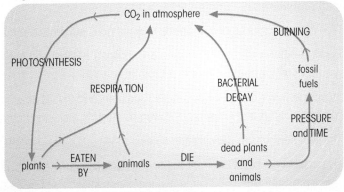

Earth and air

Test yourself

1 Why do we find cycles of material occurring in nature?

2 Name three of these cycles.

3 Explain how carbon from the atmosphere gets into the soil.

4 Explain two ways in which carbon is returned to the atmosphere.

5 How does the burning of fossil fuels affect the environment?

BBC GCSE Check and Test: Science

Earth and air

Check the facts

There are three types of rock:
- igneous   • **sedimentary**   • metamorphic

Igneous rocks

When the Earth first formed it was probably molten. As it cooled, its outer later solidified to form the first rocks, which were igneous rocks. Igneous rocks are formed whenever **molten rock** (**magma**) cools and solidifies.

Magma forms below the Earth's surface and rises. If the magma stops below the surface, it cools down slowly (over thousands or millions of years) to form rocks with large crystals (e.g. granite).

If the magma rises to the surface it erupts from volcanoes. It can explode out of volcanoes as volcanic ash or flow out as lava. Lava cools quickly (in days or weeks) to form rocks with small crystals (e.g. basalt).

rapid cooling ⟶ small crystals
slow cooling ⟶ large crystals

Sedimentary rocks

Rocks on the Earth's surface are broken up by **weathering** and **erosion** to form **sediments**.

Weathering breaks up and dissolves rock but does not move the fragments.

Rocks can be weathered by freezing and thawing, heating and cooling, root growth or attack by chemicals in air, rain or soil.

Erosion removes rock fragments, called sediment, which falls off or is moved by wind, water (rivers or the sea) or even by animals, including humans.

The sediment is then deposited in quieter conditions.

Over millions of years layers of sediments can build up. The lower, older layers are compacted and cemented together into sedimentary rock (e.g. limestone).

Metamorphic rocks

Metamorphic rocks are formed from other rocks by **great pressure** and **heat** but without melting. This happens deep below the Earth's surface when mountains are being formed. Slate is formed in this way.

Cooling magma below the surface can also cause the baking and metamorphosis of nearby rocks.

www.bbc.co.uk/revision

If the heat and pressure of mountain building is great enough, the rocks will melt to form magma that eventually becomes new igneous rock.

Evidence

Evidence for the processes by which rocks form and are recycled is not obtained directly.

You cannot observe it happening because:

- it takes too long
- it happens too deep in the Earth's crust.

The evidence is thus indirect and comes from:

- studying how sediments are formed, how volcanoes erupt and the effects of earthquakes today
- observing the features of rock in cliffs, quarries, mines and boreholes: sedimentary features, igneous features, and metamorphic features
- study of shock waves travelling through the Earth after an earthquake.

 Test yourself

1 Explain why there was only one form of rock present when the Earth first formed.

2 What is erosion?

3 Describe the formation of sedimentary rock from igneous rock.

4 Outline three ways in which evidence for the ways in which rocks are formed and recycled can be collected.

5 Explain why fossils are found in sedimentary rocks. Would the fossils in different layers be similar or different? Explain your answer.

Earth and air

BBC GCSE Check and Test: Science

Check the facts

All chemical reactions can be represented by a word **equation and a** balanced chemical equation.

Take the example of burning magnesium. The reactants are magnesium and oxygen and the product is magnesium oxide. So the word equation is:

magnesium + oxygen → magnesium oxide

The word equation indicates what happens, but tells you nothing about quantity. To get this information, you need to translate the word equation into a balanced chemical equation. This translation is a two-step process:

1 Change the word equation into symbols and formulae

$$\text{magnesium} + \text{oxygen} \rightarrow \text{magnesium oxide}$$

becomes: $Mg + O_2 \rightarrow MgO$

- Elements are written as symbols, so magnesium is Mg.
- Gaseous elements are diatomic, so oxygen is O_2.
- Compounds have a formula, so magnesium oxide is MgO.

2 Balance the symbol equation

$$Mg + O_2 \rightarrow MgO$$

becomes: $2Mg + O_2 \rightarrow 2MgO$

- Balance one symbol at a time, reading left to right.
- Put balancing numbers only at the front of a formula.
- When you have finished, go back and check your equation.

Test yourself

1 Balance the following equations:

a) $Zn + HCl \rightarrow ZnCl_2 + H_2$

b) $C + CO_2 \rightarrow CO$

c) $H_2 + O_2 \rightarrow H_2O$

d) $Al + Fe_2O_3 \rightarrow Al_2O_3 + Fe$

e) $KOH + H_2SO_4 \rightarrow K_2SO_4 + H_2O$

f) $ZnSO_4 + NaOH \rightarrow Zn(OH)_2 + Na_2SO_4$

g) $Pb(NO_3)_2 \rightarrow PbO + NO_2 + O_2$

2 Translate these word equations into balanced chemical equations:

a) copper oxide + hydrogen → copper + water

b) sodium + water → sodium hydroxide + hydrogen

c) nitrogen + hydrogen → ammonia

d) zinc carbonate → zinc oxide + carbon dioxide

e) sodium hydroxide + magnesium chloride →
magnesium hydroxide + sodium chloride

Chemical equations

www.bbc.co.uk/revision

Check the facts

A balanced chemical equation is quantitative and enables the masses of reactants and products to be calculated.

Example

Q What mass of magnesium oxide is produced by completely burning 6 g of magnesium in oxygen (relative atomic masses: $O = 16$, $Mg = 24$)?

A Equation: $\quad 2Mg \quad + \quad O_2 \quad \rightarrow \quad 2MgO$

Atomic masses: $2 \times 24 \qquad 2 \times 16 \quad \rightarrow \quad 2 \times (24 + 16)$

$$48 \qquad\qquad 32 \quad \rightarrow \quad 80$$

Ignore the oxygen as you are not asked about it.

Divide by 48: $\quad 1 \qquad\qquad\qquad \rightarrow \quad \dfrac{80}{48}$

You have 6 g of magnesium so multiply by 6.

$$6 \qquad\qquad\qquad \rightarrow \quad \dfrac{80}{48} \times 6$$

Therefore: $\quad$ 6 g Mg $\qquad\qquad \rightarrow \quad$ 10 g MgO

10 g of magnesium oxide is produced by completely burning 6 g of magnesium.

h

Test yourself

Relative atomic masses: $C = 12$, $Ca = 40$, $Cu = 64$, $H = 1$, $Na = 23$, $O = 16$.

1 In the reaction

$$CaCO_3 \xrightarrow{\text{heat}} CaO + CO_2$$

what mass of calcium oxide is produced by the complete decomposition of 10 g of calcium carbonate?

2 In the reaction

$$2H_2 + O_2 \rightarrow 2H_2O$$

what mass of oxygen is required to react completely with 1 g of hydrogen and what mass of water is produced?

3 What weight of copper carbonate must be completely decomposed to produce 4 g of copper oxide?

4 What mass of sodium must be burned completely to produce 0.62 g of sodium oxide?

h

Chemical equations

BBC GCSE Check and Test: Science

Chemical equations

Check the facts

> Whenever a pure compound is made, it always contains
> the same elements in the same fixed proportions by weight.
> This is the law of constant composition.

The law of constant composition means that formulae can be calculated.

h

Example

Q In a carefully controlled experiment, 2.4 g of magnesium was found to
produce 4.0 g of magnesium oxide. Calculate the formula of
magnesium oxide (relative atomic masses: Mg = 24, O = 16).

A Mass of magnesium oxide: 4.0 g
Mass of magnesium: 2.4 g
Hence mass of oxygen used: 1.6 g

Equation: magnesium + oxygen → magnesium oxide
Masses used: 2.4 g   1.6 g
Moles used: $\frac{2.4}{24} = 0.1$ $\frac{1.6}{16} = 0.1$

Hence magnesium reacts with oxygen in the ratio 1:1. So the formula
of magnesium oxide is MgO.

Test yourself

Relative atomic masses:
   C = 12, Cl = 35.5, Cu = 64, H = 1, Na = 23, O = 16, S = 32

h

1 4 g of hydrogen combine with 32 g of oxygen to produce water. Calculate
the formula of water.

2 2 g of hydrogen combine with 32 g of sulphur to produce hydrogen
sulphide. Calculate the formula of hydrogen sulphide.

3 4.6 g of sodium burn completely in chlorine to produce 11.7 g of sodium
chloride. Calculate the formula of sodium chloride.

4 Reduction of 4 g of copper oxide produces 3.2 g of copper. Calculate the
formula of copper oxide.

Check the facts

The first twenty elements in the periodic table

I	II	III	IV	V	VI	VII	0
							$_2$He Helium 2
			$_1$H Hydrogen 1				
$_3$Li Lithium 2.1	$_4$Be Beryllium 2.2	$_5$B Boron 2.3	$_6$C Carbon 2.4	$_7$N Nitrogen 2.5	$_8$O Oxygen 2.6	$_9$F Fluorine 2.7	$_{10}$Ne Neon 2.8
$_{11}$Na Sodium 2.8.1	$_{12}$Mg Magnesium 2.8.2	$_{13}$Al Aluminium 2.8.3	$_{14}$Si Silicon 2.8.4	$_{15}$P Phosphorus 2.8.5	$_{16}$S Sulphur 2.8.6	$_{17}$Cl Chlorine 2.8.7	$_{18}$Ar Argon 2.8.8
$_{19}$K Potassium 2.8.8.1	$_{20}$Ca Calcium 2.8.8.2						

Materials and their properties

> **The periodic table lists the elements in order of atomic number.**

> **The first 20 elements are arranged as shown on page 65.**

Elements that have the same number of electrons in their outer shell are in the same column.

 The vertical columns are **groups**. They contain elements with the same number of outer electrons and thus similar chemical properties.

 Horizontal rows are **periods**. Period 1 contains only hydrogen and helium, period 2 contains lithium to neon, period 3 sodium to argon and so on.

Elements in a period have the same configuration of electrons in their inner shell(s).

Following these first twenty, the electrons begin to use the sub-level of the third shell. This fills from eight to eighteen electrons over the next ten elements. These are the **transition metals**. They fit between group II and group III.

> **For more on electrons in atoms, see topic 36.**
> **For more on transition metals, see topic 59.**
> **The complete periodic table is shown on page 67.**

 ## Test yourself

1 What is the periodic table?

2 What is a 'group' in the periodic table?

3 What do the elements in a group have in common?

4 What is a 'period' in the periodic table?

5 What do the elements in a period have in common?

6 What is a transition metal?

The complete periodic table

I	II												III	IV	V	VI	VII	0
								H Hydrogen 1										He Helium 2
Li Lithium 3	Be Beryllium 4												B Boron 5	C Carbon 6	N Nitrogen 7	O Oxygen 8	F Fluorine 9	Ne Neon 10
Na Sodium 11	Mg Magnesium 12												Al Aluminium 13	Si Silicon 14	P Phosphorus 15	S Sulphur 16	Cl Chlorine 17	Ar Argon 18
K Potassium 19	Ca Calcium 20	Sc Scandium 21	Ti Titanium 22	V Vanadium 23	Cr Chromium 24	Mn Manganese 25	Fe Iron 26	Co Cobalt 27	Ni Nickel 28	Cu Copper 29	Zn Zinc 30		Ga Gallium 31	Ge Germanium 32	As Arsenic 33	Se Selenium 34	Br Bromine 35	Kr Krypton 36
Rb Rubidium 37	Sr Strontium 38	Y Yttrium 39	Zr Zirconium 40	Nb Niobium 41	Mo Molybdenum 42	Tc Technetium 43	Ru Ruthenium 44	Rh Rhodium 45	Pd Palladium 46	Ag Silver 47	Cd Cadmium 48		In Indium 49	Sn Tin 50	Sb Antimony 51	Te Tellurium 52	I Iodine 53	Xe Xenon 54
Cs Caesium 55	Ba Barium 56	La Lanthanum 57 x	Hf Hafnium 72	Ta Tantalum 73	W Tungsten 74	Re Rhenium 75	Os Osmium 76	Ir Iridium 77	Pt Platinum 78	Au Gold 79	Hg Mercury 80		Tl Thallium 81	Pb Lead 82	Bi Bismuth 83	Po Polonium 84	At Astatine 85	Rn Radon 86
Fr Francium 87	Ra Radium 88	Ac Actinium 89 •																

This line divides the metals from the non-metals.

x Lanthanide series

Ce Cerium 58	Pr Praseodymium 59	Nd Neodymium 60	Pm Promethium 61	Sm Samarium 62	Eu Europium 63	Gd Gadolinium 64	Tb Terbium 65	Dy Dysprosium 66	Ho Holmium 67	Er Erbium 68	Tm Thulium 69	Yb Ytterbium 70	Lu Lutetium 71

• Actinide series

Th Thorium 90	Pa Protactinium 91	U Uranium 92	Np Neptunium 93	Pu Plutonium 94	Am Americium 95	Cm Curium 96	Bk Berkelium 97	Cf Californium 98	Es Einsteinium 99	Fm Fermium 100	Md Mendelevium 101	No Nobelium 102	Lr Lawrencium 103

KEY

X
element name
z

X = atomic symbol
z = atomic number

[1] Group I comprises the alkali metals.   [2] Group II comprises the alkaline–earth metals.   [3] Group VII comprises the halogens.   [4] Group 0 comprises the noble gases.

Materials and their properties

BBC GCSE Check and Test: Science

Materials and their properties

Check the facts

Group O contains the **noble gases** which are chemically inert.

> **For more on noble gases, see topic 54.**

> **From left to right across a period there is a gradual change from the most metallic elements in group I to the most non-metallic elements in group VII.**

Moving down a metal group there is a gradual increase in metallic properties.

Moving up a non-metal group there is a gradual increase in non-metallic properties.

Thus, the most metallic elements are at the bottom left of the table and the most non-metallic are at the top right.

Test yourself

> **Refer to the periodic table in topic 52**

1 Give the name and symbol of two elements you would expect to have similar chemical properties to each of the following:
   a) sodium   b) calcium   c) sulphur   d) fluorine.

2 Where in the periodic table do you find:
   a) the most metallic element   c) elements: atomic numbers 11–18
   b) the most non-metallic element d) elements: 6 electrons in outer shell?

3 The grid shows six elements in the periodic table.
   The letters are *not* the symbols of the elements.

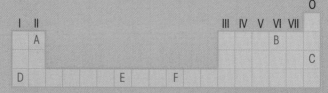

   a) Give the letters of three metals and say which is the most metallic.
   b) Give the letters of two non-metals. Which is the most non-metallic?
   c) Write the formula of the compounds formed from:
      i) D and B   ii) A and B.
   d) What do E and F have in common?
   e) Do D and A react together? Explain your answer.

Check the facts

Materials and their properties

The noble gases are found in group O of the periodic table.

Name and symbol	Atomic number	Electronic configuration	Boiling point (°C)
Helium He	2	2	−269
Neon Ne	10	2.8	−246
Argon Ar	18	2.8.8	−186
Krypton Kr	36	2.8.18.8	−153
Xenon Xe	54	2.8.18.18.8	−108
Radon Rn	86	2.8.18.32.8	−62

• All have low boiling points, increasing down the group. This is because the atom gets heavier and so the inter-atomic forces are greater.

• All have electronic configurations with complete outer shells.

These stable electronic structures mean that the noble gases are inert chemically. This means that they are monatomic, in other words, they exist as single atoms and not diatomic molecules like other gaseous elements.

Main uses of the noble gases:		
Helium	**Neon**	**Argon**
Less dense than air and does not burn, therefore used to fill airships and weather balloons.	Glows brightly when electricity is passed through it, therefore used in advertising signs.	Used to fill domestic light bulbs because its inertness prevents the filament from burning away.

Test yourself

1 Why do the boiling points of the noble gases increase down the group?

2 Why are the noble gases sometimes called the 'inert gases'?

3 Explain what is meant by 'monatomic' and why the noble gases are monatomic.

4 Explain why helium is used in weather balloons.

5 Why is argon used to fill domestic light bulbs?

BBC GCSE Check and Test: Science

Check the facts

The alkali metals are group 1 of the periodic table.

Name and symbol	Atomic number	Electronic configuration	Melting point (°C)
Lithium Li	3	2.1	180
Sodium Na	11	2.8.1	98
Potassium K	19	2.8.8.1	63.5
Rubidium Rb	37	2.8.18.8.1	39
Caesium Cs	55	2.8.18.18.8.1	29
Francium Fr	87	2.8.18.32.8.1	27

All have low melting points, decreasing down the group because the structure of the larger atoms is easier to disrupt with heat.

Reactivity increases down the group as the one outer electron, which is lost during a reaction to form the M^+ ion, is more easily lost. This is because it is further from the positive nucleus and thus less firmly held.

The alkali metals react with:	
oxygen	when burnt in air, to form oxides $4M\ (s) + O_2\ (g) \rightarrow 2M_2O\ (s)$
water	to form hydrogen plus an alkaline solution of the hydroxide $2M\ (s) + 2H_2O\ (l) \rightarrow 2MOH\ (aq) + H_2\ (g)$
group VII halogens	to form halides $2M\ (s) + X_2\ (g) \rightarrow 2MX\ (s)$

Test yourself

1 Why are the chemical reactions of the alkali metals the same throughout the group?

2 Why does reactivity increase with increasing atomic number?

3 Write the formula of the reactions between:
a) the chloride of potassium   b) the oxide of sodium
c) the hydroxide of lithium.

4 Write balanced equations and name the products for:
a) sodium and bromine   b) potassium and oxygen
c) sodium and water.

Materials and their properties

Check the facts

All alkali metal compounds are soluble in water.

> **As the alkali metals are reactive, their compounds are stable and are not decomposed by heat, but when molten they can be decomposed by electricity.**

Example

$$2NaCl \text{ (l)} \xrightarrow{\text{electrolysis}} 2Na \text{ (s)} + Cl_2 \text{ (g)}$$

All alkali metal compounds are **ionic**. For example: $NaOH \rightarrow Na^+ + OH^-$

Some uses of sodium compounds

Compound	Uses
Sodium chloride	• electrolysed in solution to produce $NaOH$, H_2 and Cl_2 in the manufacture of sodium carbonate (washing soda) • in food as a preservative
Sodium carbonate (washing soda)	• in the manufacture of glass • to soften hard water
Sodium hydroxide (caustic soda)	• in the manufacture of soaps and detergents • in paper-making • in the manufacture of ceramics

h

Test yourself

1 What happens, if anything, when sodium carbonate is heated? Explain your answer.

2 Explain how potassium could be extracted from potassium chloride.

3 Which sodium compound can be used in the production of:
 a) glass   b) soap   c) paper
 d) hydrogen   e) chlorine   f) ceramics
 g) sodium hydroxide   h) washing soda?

4 Which ions make up each of the following:

h
 a) K_2O b) $LiOH$ c) Na_2CO_3
 d) potassium sulphate   e) sodium nitrate f) potassium bromide?

Materials and their properties

The halogens are group VII of the periodic table.

Name and symbol	Atomic number	Electronic configuration	Colour and physical state at room temp	Boiling point (°C)
Fluorine F	9	2.7	pale yellow gas	−188
Chlorine Cl	17	2.8.7	green-yellow gas	−35
Bromine Br	35	2.8.18.7	dark red liquid	59
Iodine I	53	2.8.18.18.7	shiny purple solid	185
Astatine At	85	2.8.18.32.18.7	unknown	337

The halogens are coloured, getting darker down the group. They all have low melting and boiling points, increasing down the group. All are diatomic molecules – the two atoms are joined by a **covalent bond**.

Reactivity decreases down the group because the one outer electron (gained during reaction, to form the X^- ion) is gained more quickly the closer the outer shell is to the positive nucleus.

The halogens react with:		
alkali metals	to form halides	$M\,(s) + X_2\,(g) \rightarrow 2MX\,(s)$
hydrogen	to form hydrogen halides	$H_2\,(g) + X_2\,(g) \rightarrow 2HX\,(g)$

The hydrogen halides dissolve in water to form acids.

For more on reactions forming acids, see topic 62

Test yourself

1 Predict the following for astatine:
   a) colour   b) physical state at room temperature   c) boiling point.

2 Write balanced chemical equations and name the products for each of the following reactions:
   a) sodium and iodine   b)   bromine and hydrogen.

3 Outline how chlorine is made into hydrochloric acid. Give equations where appropriate.

4 The melting point of chlorine is −101°C and of bromine is −7°C. Predict the melting points of iodine and astatine.

www.bbc.co.uk/revision

Check the facts

A more reactive halogen will displace a less reactive halogen from an ionic compound solution of the less reactive halogen.

Chlorine displaces bromine from potassium bromide solution.

$$Cl_2 \text{ (g)} + 2KBr \text{ (aq)} \rightarrow Br_2 \text{ (l)} + 2KCl \text{ (aq)}$$

Bromine displaces iodine from potassium iodide solution.

$$Br_2 \text{ (l)} + 2KI \text{ (aq)} \rightarrow I_2 \text{ (s)} + 2KBr \text{ (aq)}$$

These reactions can be seen as similar to the reactivity series of metals in which the more reactive metal displaces the less reactive.

For more on reactivity, see topic 40.

Bonding in halogen compounds

The halogens form **ionic compounds** with metals:

$$MX \rightarrow M^+ + X^-$$
$$MX_2 \rightarrow M^{2+} + 2X^-$$

HCl, hydrogen chloride

Cl_2O, chlorine oxide

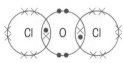

They also form **covalent molecules** with non-metals.

Test yourself

1 Write a balanced chemical equation or write 'no reaction' for each of the following pairs of reactants:
   a) chlorine and sodium bromide   b) iodine and sodium chloride
   c) bromine and sodium iodide   d) iodine and sodium bromide.

2 Which ions make up each of the following:
   a) calcium chloride   b) sodium iodide
   c) magnesium bromide   d) lithium chloride?

3 Draw diagrams to show the covalent bonding in the following:
   a) hydrogen bromide   b) diatomic bromine
   c) phosphorus trichloride (PCl_3)   d) chloric I acid (HOCl).

Check the facts

The transition metals are found in the periodic table in the block between group II and group III.

The elements in the first transition series

Name and symbol	Atomic number	Electronic configuration	Melting point (°C)
Scandium Sc	21	2.8.9.2	1540
Titanium Ti	22	2.8.10.2	1670
Vanadium V	23	2.8.11.2	1800
Chromium Cr	24	2.8.12.2	1850
Manganese Mn	25	2.8.13.2	1245
Iron Fe	26	2.8.14.2	1530
Cobalt Co	27	2.8.15.2	1490
Nickel Ni	28	2.8.16.2	1450
Copper Cu	29	2.8.17.2	1083
Zinc Zn	30	2.8.18.2	420

These metals are good conductors of electricity because the spaces in the incomplete shell allow electron movement.

They have strong inter-atomic forces and this results in high melting points.

They have similar-sized atoms because the number of electron shells in use is the same across the series.

Because of the similar electronic configurations there are many similarities across the series. This means there aren't the obvious trends seen moving down the group in the alkali metals, the halogens and the noble gases.

Unlike the metals in groups I and II (which all have white compounds that form colourless aqueous solutions) the transition metals have coloured compounds that form coloured solutions (e.g. blue copper sulphate).

Zinc is included in the series but its inner electron shells are completely filled. It therefore has white compounds which form colourless solutions.

Metals in the first transition series lose electrons and positive ions in reaction:

$$M - 2e^- \rightarrow M^{2+}$$

 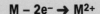

• Many of them demonstrate variable electron loss depending upon the reaction and conditions.

$$Fe - 2e^- \rightarrow Fe^{2+} \quad \text{or} \quad Fe - 3e^- \rightarrow Fe^{3+}$$

Properties and uses of transition metals

Metal	Properties	Uses
Titanium	• great strength • resistant to corrosion • light	• in aircraft • in replacement hip joints
Chromium	• extremely hard • resistant to corrosion	• used in steel alloys • plating
Iron	• not particularly hard • quite reactive	• used in steel, cast iron and wrought iron • as a catalyst in processes such as the Haber process
Copper	• malleable • ductile • resistant to corrosion • excellent conductor of heat and electricity	• used in wiring, piping, containers, etc.
Zinc	• highly resistant to corrosion • more reactive than iron so is protected even if the iron is exposed	• used to protect iron articles by coating (galvanising)

Test yourself

1 Explain why the transition metals:
   (a) are good conductors of electricity
   (b) have high melting points
   (c) have similar-sized atoms
   (d) have similar physical and chemical properties
   (e) are all metals.

2 Explain why compounds of zinc are white whilst compounds of other transition metals are coloured.

3 Explain why zinc has a low melting point compared to the other metals in the series.

Chemical reactions and rates

Check the facts

> **Both gain of oxygen and loss of hydrogen in a chemical reaction are called oxidation.**

Gain of oxygen in a chemical reaction

Example

$$H_2 \text{ (g)} + CuO \text{ (s)} \longrightarrow H_2O \text{ (g)} + Cu \text{ (s)}$$

oxidation

The provider of oxygen is the oxidising agent. This is CuO in the example.

Combustion (burning) is oxidation.

$$2Mg \text{ (s)} + O_2 \text{ (g)} \longrightarrow 2MgO \text{ (s)}$$

oxidation

The oxygen is the oxidising agent in this example.

Loss of hydrogen in a chemical reaction

Example

$$H_2S \text{ (g)} + Cl_2 \text{ (g)} \longrightarrow 2HCl \text{ (g)} + S \text{ (s)}$$

oxidation

The H_2S is oxidised to S by loss of hydrogen. The hydrogen is removed by chlorine and so chlorine is the oxidising agent.

Oxidation involving electrons

An atom is said to be oxidised when it loses electrons in a chemical reaction.

Example

$$Zn \text{ (s)} + 2HCl \text{ (aq)} \rightarrow ZnCl_2 \text{ (aq)} + H_2 \text{ (g)}$$

Each zinc atom loses two electrons in the course of the reaction.

The electrons go to the two hydrogen ions in the 2HCl.

The zinc atoms are oxidised by electron loss. This is written as:

$$Zn - 2e^- \longrightarrow Zn^{2+} \quad \text{or} \quad Zn \longrightarrow Zn^{2+} - 2e^-$$

oxidation   oxidation

Chemical reactions and rates

The hydrogen ions, the takers of the electrons, are the oxidising agent.

This explanation can also be applied to the burning of magnesium.

$$2Mg \ (s) + O_2 \ (g) \rightarrow 2MgO \ (s)$$

During the reaction, each Mg atom loses two electrons and is oxidised.

$$Mg - 2e^- \longrightarrow Mg^{2+}$$

oxidation

The electrons go to the O_2 to make it into O^{2-}; thus the O_2 is the oxidising agent.

Test yourself

1 Define oxidation in terms of both oxygen and hydrogen.

2 Explain, in terms of both oxygen and hydrogen, what an oxidising agent is.

3 In each of the following, say which material is oxidised and which material is the oxidising agent:

a) $ZnO \ (s) + C \ (s) \rightarrow ZnO \ (s) + CO \ (g)$

b) $Fe_2O_3 + 3CO \ (g) \rightarrow 2Fe \ (s) + 3CO_2 \ (g)$

c) $S \ (s) + O_2 \ (g) \rightarrow SO_2 \ (g)$

d) $Cl_2 \ (g) + 2HBr \ (aq) \rightarrow 2HCl \ (aq) + Br_2 \ (l)$

e) $CH_4 \ (g) + 2Cl_2 \ (g) \rightarrow C \ (s) + 4HCl \ (g)$

4 In each of the following, explain why the first reactant can be said to have been oxidised:

a) $4Na \ (s) + O_2 \ (g) \rightarrow 2Na_2O \ (s)$

b) $Ca \ (s) + 2H_2O \ (l) \rightarrow Ca(OH)_2 \ (aq) + H_2 \ (g)$

c) $2Na \ (s) + Cl_2 \ (g) \rightarrow 2NaCl \ (s)$

d) $Fe \ (s) + CuSO_2 \ (aq) \rightarrow FeSO_2 \ (aq) + Cu \ (s)$

In each case write an equation involving electrons in your explanation.

BBC GCSE Check and Test: Science

Check the facts

Chemical reactions and rates

> Reduction is the opposite of oxidation and is therefore:
> - loss of oxygen in a chemical reaction
> - **gain of hydrogen in a chemical reaction**
> - gain of electrons in a chemical reaction.

Loss of oxygen in a chemical reaction

Example

$$PbO\ (s) + C\ (s) \longrightarrow Pb\ (s) + CO\ (g)$$

reduction

PbO is reduced to Pb by oxygen loss. C is the reducing agent.

Gain of hydrogen in a chemical reaction

Example

$$Cl_2\ (g) + 2HI\ (aq) \longrightarrow 2HCl\ (aq) + I_2\ (s)$$

reduction

Cl_2 is reduced to HCl by hydrogen gain. HI is the reducing agent.

Gain of electrons in a chemical reaction

Example

$$2K\ (s) + Cl_2\ (g) \rightarrow 2KCl\ (s)$$

Each Cl atom gains an electron to become a Cl^- ion:

$$Cl + e^- \rightarrow Cl^-.$$

Cl_2 is reduced by electron gain. K is the reducing agent.

Redox reactions

> **Oxidation and reduction always occur together in a reaction. These reactions are called redox reactions.**

Example

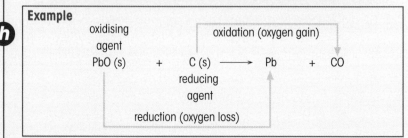

oxidising agent

oxidation (oxygen gain)

$$PbO\ (s) + C\ (s) \longrightarrow Pb + CO$$

reducing agent

reduction (oxygen loss)

reducing agent

reduction (hydrogen gain)

$$H_2S \text{ (g)} + Cl_2 \text{ (g)} \longrightarrow S + 2HCl \text{ (g)}$$

oxidising agent

oxidation (hydrogen loss)

In redox reactions, the oxidising agent is reduced and the reducing agent is oxidised. For example: $2Mg \text{ (s)} + O_2 \text{ (g)} \rightarrow 2MgO \text{ (s)}$

The two electrons lost by each Mg atom are gained by each O atom.

$$2Mg - 4e^- \rightarrow 2Mg^{2+} = \text{oxidation}$$
$$O_2 + 4e^- \rightarrow 2O^{2-} = \text{reduction}$$

These two equations are called **electron-transfer, half-reaction equations**. The balanced ionic equation for the reaction is:

oxidation (loss of electrons)

$$2Mg + O_2 \longrightarrow 2Mg^{2+} + 2O^{2-}$$

reduction (gain of electrons)

Test yourself

1 State three different ways of defining reduction.

2 $Fe_2O_3 \text{ (s)} + 2Al \text{ (s)} \rightarrow 2Fe \text{ (s)} + Al_2O_3 \text{ (s)}$
In this reaction, which material is: a) oxidised; (b) reduced;
c) the oxidising agent; (d) the reducing agent?

3 What is a redox reaction?

4 In the following reaction, what is oxidised and what reduced?

$$Cl_2 + 2Br^- \rightarrow 2Cl^- + Br_2$$

Rewrite the reaction as two electron-transfer, half-reaction equations.

5 Calcium will burn in air to form calcium oxide.
Explain, with equations, why this is a redox reaction.

BBC GCSE Check and Test: Science

62 Neutralisation

Check the facts

Neutralisation is the reaction between acids and alkalis.

All acids have pH less than 7.

0 Strong acids   Weak acids 7   Neutral

Bases are oxides and hydroxides of metals.

acid + base → salt + water

Example

H_2SO_4 (aq) + CuO (s) → $CuSO_4$ (aq) + H_2O (l)

The vast majority of bases are insoluble in water. The few that are soluble are called alkalis. The two most common alkalis are:

- sodium hydroxide, NaOH
- potassium hydroxide, KOH

Alkalis have pH greater than 7

7 Weak alkalis   Strong 14 alkalis   Neutral

Alkalis are bases and therefore react with acids.

acid + alkali → salt + water

Example

HCl (aq) + NaOH (aq) → NaCl (aq) + H_2O (l)

The pH of the acid and alkali cancel each other out.

The pH of the salt solution formed is 7 (neutral).

For this reason, the reaction between an acid and an alkali is called a neutralisation reaction.

Neutralisation reactions

 Dilute acids are excellent conductors of electricity. They must, therefore, consist mainly of ions.

Example

Dissolving hydrogen chloride gas in water to form hydrochloric acid causes ions to be produced.

$$HCl \, (g) \xrightarrow{\text{in water}} \underbrace{H^+ \, (aq) + Cl^- \, (aq)}_{\text{hydrochloric acid}}$$

The hydrogen ion (H^+) is present in all acids. It is responsible for the characteristic properties of acids.

Similarly when soluble bases are dissolved in water, hydroxide ions (OH^-) are produced.

$$NaOH \, (s) \xrightarrow{\text{in water}} \underbrace{Na^+ \, (aq) + OH^- \, (aq)}_{\text{sodium hydroxide solution}}$$

When an acid reacts with an alkali, the H^+ ions of the acid combine with the OH^- ions of the alkali to form water molecules. This is the essence of a neutralisation reaction.

The simplest ionic equation for neutralisation is:

$$H^+ \, (aq) + OH^- \, (aq) \rightarrow H_2O \, (l)$$

Test yourself

1 Give a definition of:
   a) an acid
   b) an alkali.

2 What is 'neutralisation'? Why is it given this name?

3 For the reaction between sulphuric acid and potassium hydroxide, write:
   a) a balanced chemical equation
   b) the simplest ionic equation.

4 For the reaction between potassium hydroxide and hydrochloric acid, write:
   a) a balanced chemical equation
   b) the simplest ionic equation.

5 Dilute sulphuric acid is a very good conductor of electricity whereas very concentrated sulphuric acid is a poor conductor of electricity. What does this tell you about the ionisation of sulphuric acid?

Check the facts

Decomposition is the breaking down of a compound into two or more simpler substances.

> **When this breakdown is brought about by heating, the process is called thermal decomposition.**

For example, If green copper carbonate powder is heated it decomposes easily into black copper oxide powder and carbon dioxide gas.

$$CuCO_3 \text{ (s)} \rightarrow CuO \text{ (s)} + CO_2 \text{ (g)}$$

Similarly, marble chips (calcium carbonate) decompose on heating.

$$CaCO_3 \text{ (s)} \rightarrow CaO \text{ (s)} + CO_2 \text{ (g)}$$

> **Reactive metals have stable compounds; less reactive metals have less stable compounds.**

The decomposition of calcium carbonate is much more difficult than that of copper carbonate. It requires much more heat because calcium is much more reactive than copper, so its compounds are much more stable.

The stable compounds of very reactive metals (which cannot be decomposed by heat) can often be decomposed by electricity when molten:

> **NaCl → stable, no reaction**
> **but 2NaCl (l) → 2Na (s) + Cl$_2$ (g)**

Test yourself

1 What is meant by 'decomposition'?

2 What is meant by 'thermal decomposition'?

3 Write a balanced equation for the thermal decomposition of magnesium carbonate and name all the products.

4 Explain why sodium carbonate will not decompose when heated.

5 Potassium chloride will not decompose when heated.
   a) What does this tell you about potassium?
   b) How could potassium chloride be decomposed?
      Write an equation for the reaction.

Check the facts

Enzymes are proteins contained in the human body. They catalyse the body's chemical reactions.

Each enzyme is specific and catalyses one reaction. A living cell may contain a thousand enzymes.

Catalysts alter rates of a reaction but are not chemically changed.

Examples

Amylase	found in saliva; catalyses conversion of starch to sugars
Pysozyme	catalyses the breakdown of sugars in bacteria, which destroys the bacteria

Enzymes work by fitting into the reactant molecule like a jigsaw piece. They will not fit into any other molecule.

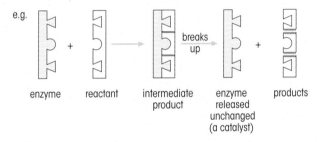

e.g.

| enzyme | reactant | intermediate product | enzyme released unchanged (a catalyst) | products |

Enzymes are pH- and temperature-sensitive. They work best at 40°C / pH 6.5. There is a rapid decline in effectiveness outside 35–45°C / pH 6.0–7.0.

Enzymes are widely used in industry, for example, in fermentation, cheese making, pharmaceuticals manufacture and vitamin production. Their most familiar use is in biological washing powders. Enzymes, called proteases, break down proteins in the stains, such as oil, dirt, gravy and blood.

Test yourself

1 What are enzymes and where are they found?

2 What function do enzymes fulfil?

3 How do enzymes work?

4 Name two enzymes.

5 Why are some washing powders described as 'biological'? How do they work?

Chemical reactions and rates

BBC GCSE Check and Test: Science

Check the facts

Chemical reactions and rates

Scientists use the study of materials and their reactions to find rules and patterns that enable predictions to be made.

Types of reaction

Knowing about **combustion**, **redox reactions**, **decomposition** and reactions of **acids** and **alkalis** enables you to predict behaviours.

Q What happens when sodium is burned in air?

A Burning (combustion) means combining with oxygen, therefore sodium oxide will be formed:

$$4Na \text{ (s)} + O_2 \text{ (g)} \rightarrow 2Na_2O \text{ (s)}$$

Q What happens when dilute sulphuric acid reacts with magnesium?

A When an acid reacts with a metal:

$$acid + metal \rightarrow salt + hydrogen$$

therefore:

$$H_2SO_4 \text{ (aq)} + Mg \text{ (s)} \rightarrow MgSO_4 \text{ (aq)} + H_2 \text{ (g)}$$

Q What happens when zinc carbonate is heated?

A When the compounds of the less reactive metals are heated alone they decompose, therefore

$$ZnCO_3 \text{ (s)} \xrightarrow{\text{heat}} ZnO \text{ (s)} + CO_2 \text{ (g)}$$

For more on reactions, see topics 60–63.

The reactivity series of metals

Knowing the position of a metal in the reactivity series allows you to predict:

- how it will react with air, water and acids
- if it will displace another metal from solution
- how easy or difficult it will be to extract from its ores and how this will best be done.

For more on reactivity, see topic 40.

The periodic table

Knowing the position of an element in the periodic table gives information about its physical and chemical properties.

Chemical reactions and rates

Q Element X has atomic number 12. What predictions can you make about the element from this?

A Atomic number 12 means 12 protons and therefore 12 electrons in atoms of X. This gives an electronic configuration of 2.8.2. The element therefore:
- is in group II of the periodic table
- will have the physical properties of metals, that is, high melting point, conductor of heat and electricity, etc.
- will have the chemical properties of metals, that is, will burn in air, react with acids, form ionic compounds, etc.

- is a metal which reacts by losing two electrons to form X^{2+} ions.

For more on the periodic table, see topic 52.

Test yourself

1 Predict the word equation and write a balanced chemical equation for:
   a) the combustion of zinc powder
   b) the reaction of copper oxide with hydrogen.

2 Element Y has an atomic number of 8.
   a) What is its electronic configuration?
   b) To which group of the periodic table does it belong?
   c) Is it a metal or a non-metal?
   d) Will it form ions? If so, write the symbol of the ions formed.
   e) Will it react with hydrogen? If it does, will the compound formed be ionic or covalent? Explain your answer.

3 Zinc is above copper but below magnesium in the reactivity series. For each of the following pairs write the word equation if you predict they react and 'no reaction' if you predict they will not:
   a) magnesium and zinc sulphate solution
   b) copper and zinc sulphate solution
   c) zinc and copper sulphate solution
   d) copper and magnesium sulphate solution.

BBC GCSE Check and Test: Science

Chemical reactions and rates

Check the facts

> Reactions proceed at different rates. An explosion is a very fast reaction. Rusting is a very slow reaction.

The **collision theory** states that for reactant particles to react together they must:

- collide with each other
- collide with sufficient energy to react rather than just bounce away – this is **activation energy**.

Conditions which change the number of occurrences of the above collisions, change the rate of the reaction. That is, the rate of a reaction is dependent on the number of fruitful collisions per unit time.

Temperature and rate

Heating particles gives them energy hence they move faster and collide more often. Because the collisions are at higher energy levels, more are fruitful. So rate increases as temperature increases.

Concentration and rate

If one or more of the reactants is in solution, then increasing the concentration increases the number of particles available.

This will increase the number of fruitful collisions and hence rate.

Example

$$Mg\ (s) + 2HCl\ (aq) \rightarrow MgCl_2\ (aq) + H_2\ (g)$$

If the hydrochloric acid solution is dilute, the reaction will be much slower than if it were concentrated.

Hence rate increases as concentration increases.

Surface area and rate

Reactions involving solids are much faster if the solid is used in small pieces or is powdered.

Example

$$CaCO_3\ (s) + 2HCl\ (aq) \rightarrow CaCl_2\ (aq) + H_2O\ (l) + CO_2\ (g)$$

This reaction is much faster if smaller pieces of marble chip are used. Powdered marble chip reacts very quickly.

This is because when the solid is powdered far more atoms are exposed to the acid and hence the number of fruitful collisions increases.

Rate increases with increasing surface area.

Catalyst

Some reactions can be speeded up by adding a catalyst.

The catalyst does not increase the number of collisions, but works by reducing the activation energy needed for fruitful collisions.

> **A catalyst alters the rate of a reaction without itself being changed in any way.**

The graph below shows this:

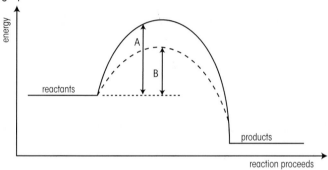

Test yourself

1 Apart from explosions and rusting, give an example of:
  a) a fast reaction
  b) a slow reaction.

2 According to the collision theory, what are the requirements for particles to react?

3 Catalysts can be used to slow down reactions. They are then called inhibitors. How do you think they might work?

BBC GCSE Check and Test: Science

Chemical reactions and rates

Check the facts

> **Most chemical reactions become either hotter or colder as they proceed. These temperature changes are associated with energy changes when bonds are broken or made.**

Reactions begin by breaking the bonds between atoms in the reactants. To do this, energy must be put in.

New products form bonds and energy is released.

> **Breaking bonds, energy in.**
> **Making bonds, energy out.**

If less energy has to be put in to break reactant bonds than is given out when making product bonds, then, overall, energy is released from the reaction. This is an exothermic reaction.

If more energy is needed to break bonds than is released in making bonds, then, overall, energy is used by the reaction. This is an endothermic reaction.

The energy changes associated with chemical reactions can be represented on **energy level diagrams**.

(h) Exothermic reactions

Here the energy content of the reactants is greater than the energy content of the products.

More energy is given out in bond formation than is used in bond breaking.

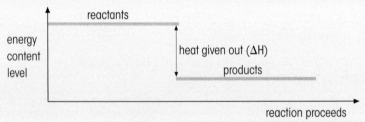

Endothermic reactions

Here the situation is exactly the reverse of the above.

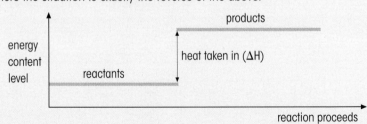

The heat of reaction

The heat change is called the heat of reaction and has the symbol ΔH which means change in heat.

ΔH is measured in kilojoules per mole (kJ/mole).

In exothermic reactions	the change in heat is downwards and ΔH is negative
In endothermic reactions	the change in heat is upwards and ΔH is positive

Test yourself

1 The equation for the burning of natural gas (methane, CH_4) is:

$$CH_4 \text{ (g)} + 2O_2 \text{ (g)} \rightarrow CO_2 \text{ (g)} + 2H_2O \text{ (g)}$$

Heat is given out and therefore the reaction is exothermic.

a) Which has the greater heat content, methane and oxygen, or carbon dioxide and steam?

b) Draw a labelled energy level diagram for this reaction.

c) Is ΔH positive or negative? Explain your answer.

2 When nitrogen and hydrogen make ammonia the equation is:

$$N_2 \text{ (g)} + 3H_2 \text{ (g)} \rightarrow 2NH_3 \text{ (g)}$$

a) Which and how many bonds have to be broken?

b) Which and how many bonds are formed?

c) ΔH is negative for this reaction. Explain fully what this tells you about the energy changes associated with the reaction.

3 Given that:

$H_2 \text{ (g)} \rightarrow 2H \text{ (g)}$	$\Delta H = +436 \text{ kJ/mole}$
$Br_2 \text{ (g)} \rightarrow 2Br \text{ (g)}$	$\Delta H = +224 \text{ kJ/mole}$
$H \text{ (g)} + Br \text{ (g)} \rightarrow HBr \text{ (g)}$	$\Delta H = -366 \text{ kJ/mole}$

a) Calculate ΔH for the reaction

$$H_2 \text{ (g)} + Br_2 \text{ (g)} \rightarrow 2HBr \text{ (g)}$$

b) Is this reaction exothermic or endothermic?

Check the facts

Ammonia is manufactured in the Haber process.

$$N_2 \text{ (g)} + 3H_2 \text{ (g)} \rightarrow 2NH_3 \text{ (g)}$$

The process is affected by ammonia being easily decomposed.

$$2NH_3 \text{ (g)} \rightarrow N_2 \text{ (g)} + 3H_2 \text{ (g)}$$

This means the reaction can go in either direction. It is **reversible**. The reaction is exothermic and the complete equation is:

$$N_2 \text{ (g)} + 3H_2 \text{ (g)} \rightleftharpoons 2NH_3 \text{ (g)} \quad \Delta H \text{ is negative}$$

In a reversible reaction both forward and backward reactions take place simultaneously.

When the rate of the forward reaction equals the rate of the backward reaction there is no change in the amounts of the reactants and products. At this point, the reaction has reached equilibrium.

The **position of equilibrium** tells you how much of the reactants and products are present at equilibrium. E.g. there may be 20% NH_3 : 80% N_2/H_2 at equilibrium, or 40% NH_3 : 60% N_2/H_2, etc. The position of equilibrium can be changed by changing the conditions of the reaction.

Le Chatelier's principle states that the equilibrium will move to oppose change. It predicts the effect on equilibrium position by changing conditions.

1 Increasing temperature

- Le Chatelier's principle says the system will try to absorb the heat. The backward reaction is favoured and there is a decrease in ammonia yield.
- This will increase the number of collisions and hence rate.
- High temperature therefore means high rate but low yield.

2 Increasing pressure

- Le Chatelier's principle says the system will absorb the increase by going to smaller volume. The forward reaction is favoured because there are fewer molecules on the right of the equation.
- Molecules will be pushed closer together, increasing collisions and rate.
- High pressure means high rate and high yield.

3 Catalyst

- Using a catalyst will not affect the position of equilibrium but will increase rate.

Summary

The conditions usually chosen to give the best compromise between yield, rate and cost are:

$$N_2 \text{ (g)} + 3H_2 \text{ (g)} \xrightarrow[\substack{500\text{--}550°C \\ \text{Fe catalyst}}]{250 \text{ atmospheres}} 2NH_3 \text{ (g)}, \Delta H \text{ is negative}$$

This yields about 15% conversion at equilibrium.

The contact process

Another example of a reversible industrial process is the contact process for the manufacture of sulphuric acid.

Part of this process involves the reaction

$$2SO_2 \text{ (g)} + O_2 \text{ (g)} \rightleftharpoons 2SO_3 \text{ (g)}, \Delta H \text{ is negative}$$

> **For more on sulphuric acid, see topic 45.**

Test yourself

1 What is a reversible reaction?

2 What is meant by 'equilibrium'?

3 What is meant by 'position of equilibrium'?

4 Nitrogen and hydrogen are left to reach equilibrium in a sealed container. What will be the effect on the position of equilibrium of:

a) increasing temperature
b) increasing container size
c) inserting a catalyst
d) removing ammonia
e) removing nitrogen?

Explain your answers.

Check the facts

Electric current transfers energy round a circuit.

Electric current is the flow of charge, measured in amps (A).

Electric current is measured with an **ammeter**, which is placed in the circuit in series.

The current is the same all the way round a series circuit.

In a parallel circuit the current flowing into a junction is the same as the current flowing out.

0.8 A ▾   ▴0.8 A
       0.5 A
0.3 A ▾

A current only passes through a component or wire if there is a voltage across it.

Voltage is measured by placing a voltmeter in parallel with a component.

Voltage tells us the difference in the energy carried by the charge between two points.

Test yourself

1 Draw a circuit to measure the current through a lamp. Add a voltmeter to your circuit to measure the voltage across the lamp.

2 Write down the current passing points A and B in the circuit shown below.

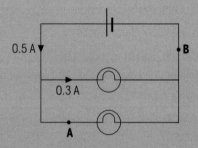

0.5 A ▾   • B

0.3 A ▸

A

3 A battery supplies 150 coulombs in 5 minutes.

a) What was the current in the circuit?

The current supplied 900 joules in 5 minutes.

b) What was the voltage of the battery?

h

Check the facts

**Changing the resistance in the circuit changes the current.
Increasing the resistance decreases the current.**

Resistance is measured in **ohms** (Ω).

$$\text{resistance } (\Omega) = \frac{\text{voltage (volts)}}{\text{current (amps)}}$$

It is also useful to think of this equation as:

$$\text{voltage (volts)} = \text{current (amps)} \times \text{resistance } (\Omega)$$
$$V = IR$$

Connecting wires need to have low resistance.

Some wires are designed to have resistance:

- the longer the wire, the greater the resistance
- the thinner the wire, the greater the resistance

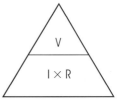

Electricity and magnetism

Test yourself

1 Write down the equation that links voltage, current and resistance.

2 In the circuit a current of 2 A passes through the 5 Ω resistor.
Calculate the voltage across the resistor.

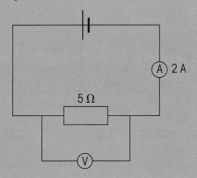

3 A variable resistor is used to change the current through a lamp.
   a) Draw a circuit to show how the lamp, variable resistor and battery
      should be connected.
   b) Explain why the lamp's brightness increases when the current increases.

h 4 A resistor has 12 V across it when 0.25 A passes through it. Calculate the
   value of the resistance.

BBC GCSE Check and Test: Science

Check the facts

Electricity and magnetism

> Components are included in circuits to control the current.

A **current–voltage graph** shows how the current in a component changes as the voltage across it changes.

A **resistor** at constant temperature has a constant resistance.

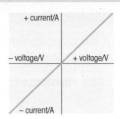

The filament in a lamp becomes hotter as the voltage across it increases. As it becomes hotter, its resistance increases.

A **diode** only allows current to pass one way. When the voltage is reversed no current passes through it.

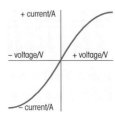

The resistance of a **thermistor** changes with temperature. The resistance of the thermistor decreases as the temperature increases. Thermistors are used to detect temperature changes.

The resistance of a **light dependent resistor** (**LDR**) decreases as the light level increases.

> For component symbols used in circuits, see page 134.

Test yourself

1 Describe how the resistance of a lamp changes as the current in the lamp increases.

2 Describe how the current through a diode changes as the voltage rises from −5 V to +5 V.

3 a) What happens to the resistance of an LDR in a circuit as the light gets brighter?

h

    b) What effect will this have on the current in the circuit?

www.bbc.co.uk/revision

Check the facts

Batteries, solar cells and generators are all sources of energy. Electric current transfers the energy from the source to the circuit.

Resistors become warm when a **current** passes through them.

The rate at which energy is transferred to the circuit is the **power**.

Power is measured in watts (W) and kilowatts (kW).
1 kW = 1000 W

You calculate electrical power using the following equation:

power (watts) = voltage (volts) × current (amps)

You calculate the energy transferred using the following equation:

energy transferred (joules) = power (watts) × time (seconds)

Test yourself

1 An immersion heater is connected to a 12 V supply. The current in the circuit is 3 A. The heater operates for 5 minutes.

　a) Calculate the power transferred from the supply to the circuit.

　b) Calculate the energy transferred from the supply to the heater in 5 minutes.

h 　c) Calculate the resistance of the heater.

2 A vacuum cleaner connected to the mains supply is rated at 2 kW and operates from the 230 V mains supply.

　a) What is 2 kW in watts?

　b) How much energy would be transferred from the mains supply to the vacuum cleaner in 10 minutes?

h 　c) What would be the current in the vacuum cleaner circuit?

Electricity and magnetism

BBC GCSE Check and Test: Science

Check the facts

The current from batteries is a **direct current** (**d.c.**). It always flows in the same direction and does not change in size.

Mains electricity supplies an **alternating current** (**a.c.**). The current is constantly changing size and direction. The direction changes fifty times per second; the frequency is 50 Hz.

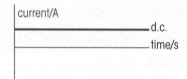

Current from a battery　　　　**Alternating current**

Electric current is supplied to the home through the live wire and returns through the neutral wire. In normal use the earth wire does not carry a current.

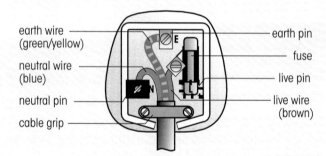

The wires in the mains cable are insulated to make sure that no current passes between the live, neutral and earth wires.

Fuses and circuit breakers are designed to break the circuit if the current is too big. This prevents damage to appliances and stops wiring overheating.

If there is a fault in an appliance and the metal part becomes live a large current might pass through you to reach earth if you are touching it at the time. For this reason the metal parts of most appliances are connected to the earth wire . This way, the large current will blow the fuse or trip the circuit breaker.

A circuit breaker will cut the circuit more quickly than a fuse.

Electricity and magnetism

www.bbc.co.uk/revision

Some appliances have plastic casing with no metal showing. The plastic insulation provides protection from an electric shock. The appliance is double insulated so it doesn't need an earth wire.

> **The energy you use has to be paid for. An electricity meter measures the energy used in kilowatt-hours (kWh).**

You can calculate the energy used by an appliance using the equation:

> **energy (kilowatt-hours) = power (kW) × time (hours)**

The electricity bill tells you the cost of a unit of electricity, which is currently about 8 pence per unit.

Test yourself

1 A lamp is rated at 250 W. What is this power rating in kW?

2 a) How much energy, in kWh, is used by a 2 kW fire if it is switched on for 3 hours?

   b) What is the cost of using the fire if the price of electricity is 8 pence per unit?

3 Explain how a fuse helps to prevent fire caused by electrical faults.

4 Explain why a double insulated device does not need an earth wire.

5 An electric iron is rated at 2.3 kW. and connected to a 230 V supply.

   a) What current will flow in the circuit when the iron is warming up?

   b) What fuse rating should be used with the iron: 1 A, 5 A or 13 A? Give a reason for your answer.

Electricity and magnetism

Check the facts

Some materials when rubbed together become charged. **Electrons** have been transferred from one material to the other. If the materials are **insulators** the charge does not leak away. This is also called **static charge**.

The object that loses electrons will be **positively charged**. The object that gains electrons will be **negatively charged**.

Two objects with the same charge repel each other.

Two objects with different charges attract each other.

An electric current is a flow of charge.
In a wire an electric current is a flow of electrons.

When molten or dissolved, some chemical compounds conduct electricity. The electric current in an **electrolyte** is carried by positive and negative ions.

For more on ions, see topic 39.

h electric charge (coulombs) = current (amps) × time (seconds)

Test yourself

1 When Jon rubs two balloons on his jumper, they gain electrons.

   a) What is the charge on the balloons called?

   b) Is the charge on Jon's jumper positive or negative?

   c) Draw a diagram to show what happens when the two balloons hang down. Explain your answer.

2 Explain why your hair might stand on end when you've pulled a jumper over your head. Use your ideas about electric charge in your answer.

3 A battery is connected to a 36 W lamp for 5 minutes. The current in the circuit is 3 A.

   a) Calculate how much charge passes through the lamp in 5 minutes.

   b) Calculate how much energy is transferred from the battery to the lamp in 5 minutes.

   c) How much energy does each coulomb of charge carry to the lamp?

   d) What is the voltage of the battery?

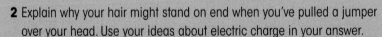

h

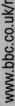

Check the facts

Electric charge is used to remove ash from the smoke in a coal-fired power station.

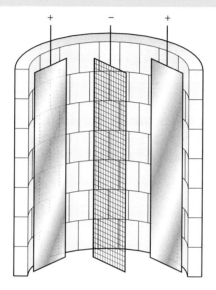

The ash particles have **positive** and **negative ions** attached. The particles are attracted to **electrodes** in the chimney.

Petrol passing along an aircraft refuelling pipe causes enough friction to give the pipe a static charge.

If the charge builds up there is a danger of sparking and explosion. The pipe is connected to earth so that the charge can leak away safely.

Test yourself

1 Explain why you sometimes get an electric shock when you touch a door handle after walking across a carpet.

2 Why does dust collect on a television screen more than elsewhere in rooms?

h **3** Explain why a charged balloon can be made to stick to a wall.

Electricity and magnetism

BBC GCSE Check and Test: Science

Electricity and magnetism

Check the facts

When a current-carrying wire is at right angles to a **magnetic field** there is a force on the wire.

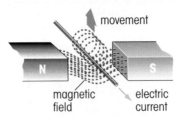

movement

magnetic field

electric current

N   S

There is a magnetic field round a wire that carries an **electric current**, which interacts with the field due to the magnets. The wire is forced upwards. The field, the wire and the force are all at right angles.

A simple electric motor has a coil of wire in a magnetic field. When a current flows the motor spins.

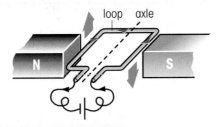

loop   axle

N   S

Test yourself

1 Complete the following sentences.

To make the force on the wires bigger and the motor spin faster you can make the current _____; or have _____ turns on the coil or use _____ magnets.

To make the force move the wire in the opposite direction you can reverse the _____ or reverse the _____.

h **2** Use your ideas about the forces on wires in magnetic fields to explain why the coil in a simple motor spins when a current passes through it.

Check the facts

Moving a magnet into a coil produces a voltage across the ends of the coil.

When the magnet is pulled out the voltage is reversed. When the magnet is stationary there is no voltage.

This effect is called **electromagnetic induction**.

Electromagnetic induction also takes place in a transformer.

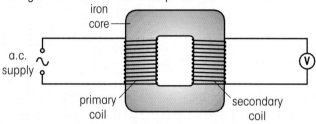

A changing current in the primary coil makes a changing magnetic field in the iron core. A changing magnetic field in the iron core induces a changing voltage across the terminals of the secondary coil. The greater the number of turns on the secondary coil the greater the voltage induced.

$$\frac{\text{voltage across primary}}{\text{voltage across secondary}} = \frac{\text{number of turns in primary coil}}{\text{number of turns in secondary coil}}$$

Test yourself

1 The north pole of a magnet is pushed into a coil and the needle on a voltmeter across the ends of the coil 'flicks' to the right.

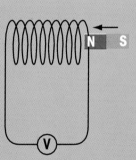

What does the needle do when:

a) the magnet remains still inside the coil
b) the magnet's north pole is pulled out of the coil
c) the magnet's south pole is pushed into the coil
d) the magnet's south pole is pulled out of the coil
e) the magnet's south pole is pushed into the other end of the coil?

2 Explain why a transformer only works when there is an alternating current (a.c.) in the primary coil.

3 A transformer is connected to a 300 V supply. There are 1200 turns on the primary coil and 40 turns on the secondary coil. What is the output from the secondary coil?

Electricity and magnetism

BBC GCSE Check and Test: Science

Check the facts

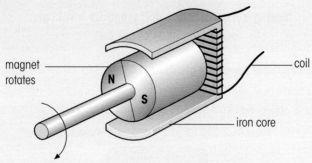

magnet rotates

coil

iron core

A magnet spinning near a coil induces a **voltage** in the coil. This voltage is enough to light a lamp. A bicycle dynamo works just like this.

> **The faster a magnet is spun, the greater the voltage induced. The more turns in the coil, the greater the voltage induced.**

Scale up the spinning magnet by replacing it with an electromagnet and you have the generator for a power station.

> **Electricity is generated in power stations.**

In most power stations **fossil fuels** are burned to heat water to make steam which turns turbines.

The turbines spin the generators that produce electricity.

> **The electricity is carried around the country through a network of cables, the National Grid.**

Cables are good **conductors** but are very long and have some **resistance**. As electricity passes through the cables they warm and lose some energy.

The greater the current, the greater the energy loss in the wires.

To reduce energy losses transformers are used to step up the electricity to a high voltage and low current.

Before the electricity is supplied to a town it is stepped down to 230 V.

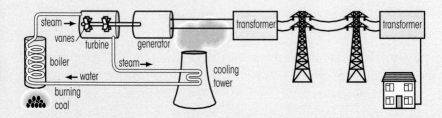

steam → vanes turbine generator transformer transformer

boiler steam → cooling tower

← water

burning coal

Test yourself

1 Why is the spinning magnet in a cycle dynamo like a magnet being pushed in and out of a coil?

2 Explain why using transformers to step up the transmission voltage means the mains electricity supply is a.c.

3 We depend on fossil fuels for our electricity supply. Suggest three reasons why we should look for alternative energy sources.

4 Look at the diagram at the bottom of the previous page. Describe three places where energy is lost between burning the coal and the energy delivered to the house.

5 A power station generates 200 MW of electrical power at 25 000 V.

a) Calculate the current in the cables.

A transformer steps the voltage up to 400 000 V.

b) Calculate the new current in the cables if there is no energy lost in the transformer.

h

Electricity and magnetism

Check the facts

If an object moves in a straight line, the average speed of the object can be calculated using an equation.

average speed (m/s) = $\dfrac{\text{distance travelled (m)}}{\text{time taken (s)}}$

distance

speed x time

Speed is measured in **metres per second** (m/s).

A **distance–time graph** for a cycle ride tells you about the journey. The steeper the graph, the shorter the time the cyclist took to cover the distance, so the faster the cyclist was moving.

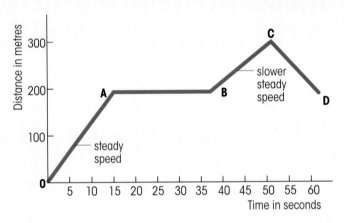

The **velocity** of an object tells us the direction as well as the speed of the moving object.

Example

An air-traffic controller needs to know the direction in which an aircraft is moving as well as its speed.

Test yourself

1 A car travels 500 metres in 20 seconds. What is its average speed?

2 Look at the distance–time graph for a cyclist above.

    a) Calculate the average speed between O and A.

    b) What do you think happened between A and B?

    c) Calculate the average speed between B and C.

    d) What happened to the cyclist between C and D?

Check the facts

> Acceleration tells you how much the velocity of an object changes each second.

You can calculate acceleration using the equation:

$$\text{acceleration (m/s}^2) = \frac{\text{change in velocity (m/s)}}{\text{time taken (s)}}$$

You measure acceleration in **metres per second every second (m/s^2)**.

A **velocity–time graph** can give you information about a bus journey. The steeper the line, the greater the change in velocity during that time, so the greater the acceleration.

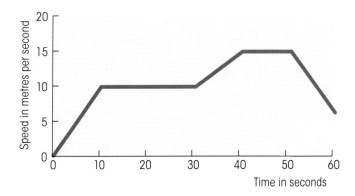

Test yourself

1 In some data about cars one car is listed as going from 0 m/s to 30 m/s in 6 seconds. What is the average acceleration?

2 Look at the velocity–time graph for the bus. Describe the journey, saying whether the bus is accelerating, decelerating or moving at a steady speed. Give as much information as you can about the journey.

3 A rocket accelerates away from its launch pad and after 5 seconds it is moving at 40 m/s. What is its average acceleration?

4 A car moves off with an average acceleration of 2.5 m/s^2 for 8 seconds. How fast will it be moving after this time?

Check the facts

Gravitational forces are felt near any massive object, such as the Sun, Moon or other planets.

The force of **gravity** on an object is its **weight**.

The weight of an object depends on its mass and the strength of the gravitational field.

Weight is a force and is measured in **newtons** (**N**).

> **weight = mass × gravitational field strength**
> **(N)   (kg)   (N/kg)**
>
> $$W = mg$$

Frictional forces resist the movement of the object over a surface or through a liquid or gas.

> **When two objects are in contact they exert equal and opposite forces on each other. Forces come in pairs.**

Example
When you sit on a chair, you push down on the cushion, compressing the springs in the cushion; the cushion pushes up on you. If it didn't, you would fall through the chair onto the floor! 

When the forces on an object are balanced, the object will remain as it is: stationary or moving at a steady speed in a straight line.

When the forces on an object are unbalanced, the object might:
• start to move in the direction of the force
• speed up (accelerate) or slow down (decelerate)
• change direction.

When an unbalanced force acts on an object to make it accelerate:
• the greater the force, the greater the acceleration
• the greater the mass, the smaller the acceleration.

To calculate the effect of a force on an object you can use this equation:

force (N) = mass (kg) × acceleration (m/s^2)
$$F = ma$$

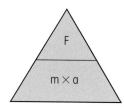

You can use arrows to show the direction of the force and its size. The longer the arrow, the greater the force.

 Test yourself

1 Look at the pictures below. The arrows show the direction and relative size of the forces acting on each object. Write down whether you think each object is accelerating, decelerating or moving at a steady speed.

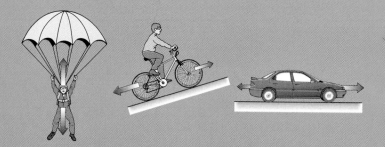

2 A car of mass 1500 kg accelerates from 0 m/s to 20 m/s in 10 seconds.

a) Calculate the acceleration of the car.

b) Calculate the force needed to give this acceleration.

3 A cyclist and her bike have a total mass of 80 kg. What force is needed to give an acceleration of 0.5 m/s^2?

4 An aircraft with a mass of 12 000 kg needs an acceleration of 3 m/s^2 to reach take-off speed before the end of the runway. What is the unbalanced force needed to give this acceleration?

Forces and motion

BBC GCSE Check and Test: Science

Forces and motion

Check the facts

> **The force needed to stop a car depends on the speed of the car and the mass of the car plus its occupants.**

The **braking distance** is the distance a car travels between the time when the brakes are applied and when the car comes to a halt.

The **thinking distance** is the distance a car travels between the time when the driver realises the brakes must be applied and when the brakes actually go on. The thinking distance depends on the speed of the car and the reaction time of the driver.

When a car has a head-on collision with a concrete bollard, both will be damaged. The car exerts a force on the bollard. The bollard exerts an equal and opposite force on the car. This is an example of forces coming in pairs.

Test yourself

1 A car is travelling at 30 m/s. The driver has a reaction time of 0.5 s. Calculate the thinking distance at this speed.

2 What would be the effect on this thinking distance if the driver were tired? Explain your answer.

3 The braking distance required for this car to slow down from 30 m/s to 0 m/s is 64 m, what is the total stopping distance?

4 Explain the effect on the stopping distance if the road was wet.

5 If the car runs into a bollard, the stopping time would be shorter. Would the stopping force be greater or smaller than the braking force? Explain your answer.

6 How would the stopping force be different if the bollard were replaced with a cushioned wall of tyres?

Check the facts

An object falls because gravity pulls it.

The force of gravity gives the object an acceleration. This is called the **acceleration due to gravity** (*g*).

On Earth $g = 9.8\,m/s^2$. (You can usually use $g = 10\,m/s^2$ in calculations.)

When objects fall through air, there is also air **resistance** acting on them.

The amount of **air resistance** depends on how fast the object is falling and the shape of the object.

As a falling object speeds up its air resistance also increases until, eventually, the pull of gravity (its weight) is balanced by the air resistance. It stops accelerating and falls at a steady speed, called its **terminal velocity**.

The greater the weight of the object, the greater the air resistance needs to be to balance it.

Test yourself

1 Complete the following sentences.

A falling object is pulled towards the Earth by _____. This force is called the _____ of the object. An object falling through air will experience air resistance. Air resistance depends on the _____ of the object and its _____ . When the air resistance is equal to the weight of the object the object will stop _____ and will move at a steady _____ , called its terminal velocity.

2 Look at the pictures of the falling parachutist.

a) Describe how the speed of the parachutist will change as she falls.

b) Suggest what difference it would make to the motion of the parachutist if she weighed a lot less.

Forces and motion

BBC GCSE Check and Test: Science

Check the facts

There are many kinds of wave: light waves, sound waves, waves on water and waves along a rope.

> **All waves carry energy; all have properties in common including reflection, refraction and diffraction.**

When a wave hits a barrier, it is reflected back. You see exactly the same effect when light is reflected from a mirror.

The **angle of incidence** is equal to the **angle of reflection**.

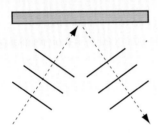

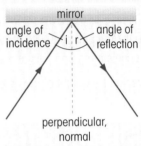

When a water wave passes into shallower water, it is slowed down. This makes the wave change direction. This is called refraction.

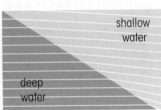

You see exactly the same effect when light passes from air into water or glass. As light slows down, it is refracted towards the normal.

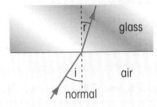

As light moves from glass to air, it speeds up, refracting away from the normal.

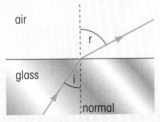

As the angle of incidence inside the glass increases, the amount of light refracted out decreases and more is reflected back inside the glass.

At the **critical angle** the light is refracted through 90° and does not emerge. At angles greater than the critical angle, the light is **totally internally reflected**.

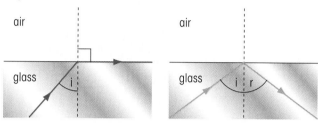

When waves pass through a gap in a barrier, they spread out on the other side. This is called diffraction.

The spreading happens best when the size of the gap is about the same size as the wavelength of the wave.

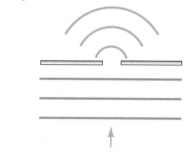

Test yourself

1 Give an example of evidence that sound waves are reflected from hard surfaces.

2 Give an example of light changing direction as it passes from one medium to another.

3 Complete the ray diagram to show how total internal reflection is used to make these two prisms into a periscope.

Check the facts

The wavelength (λ) of a wave is the distance from the crest of one wave to the crest of the next wave.

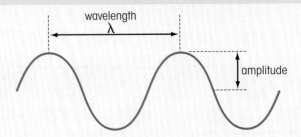

The frequency (f) of a wave is the number of waves produced each second. The unit of frequency is hertz (Hz).

The amplitude of a wave is the height of the wave from the crest to the mid-point where there is no displacement.

Wave speed (m/s) = frequency (Hz) × wavelength (m)
$$V = f\lambda$$

When one end of a rope is moved up and down, the rest of the rope begins to do so as well. Energy is transmitted down the rope, creating **transverse waves**. The energy travels along the rope but the rope moves up and down.

If a coil is pushed back and forth, energy moves along in **longitudinal waves**.

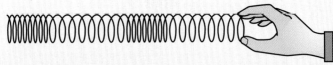

The movement of the spring is in the same direction as the travelling energy.

Test yourself

1 Group the following waves into longitudinal and transverse waves:

light waves   sound waves   water waves   waves along a rope

2 Describe how to use a cork and a stone to show that waves on water transfer energy but not matter.

3 A loudspeaker makes a sound with a frequency of 165 Hz. The wavelength of the sound is 2 m. Calculate the speed of sound.

Waves

www.bbc.co.uk/revision

Check the facts

When a ruler is set vibrating, the air ahead of the ruler is made to vibrate.

The particles in the air transmit a sound wave through the air. This is a **longitudinal wave**.

The energy carried by the wave causes your eardrum to vibrate and you hear the sound.

Sound waves reflect well off hard surfaces.

This is why you hear echoes.

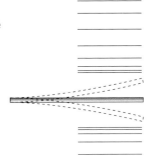

Example

Bats use echoes to locate their food and to avoid flying into obstacles. Bats use sounds at frequencies above 20 000 Hz. These frequencies are too high for humans to hear.

Very high frequencies are called ultrasound.

Ultrasound is also used for 'looking' inside human bodies. The waves are reflected from internal organs and a computer is used to build up a picture of the inside of the body.

Test yourself

1 Sound cannot travel through a vacuum. Explain why this is so.

2 A rubber band is set into vibration and makes 500 vibrations in 10 seconds. What is the frequency of the sound?

3 A bat sends out a signal. The signal's reflection returns from a moth 0.1 seconds later. The moth was 15 metres away. What is the speed of the sound?

h **4** Sound can be diffracted through gaps. Suggest some evidence that shows this. (Think about how you hear what is happening in other rooms in your house.)

Waves

Check the facts

short wavelength 0.1×10^{-11} m high frequency 10^{20} Hz	**gamma rays**	• emitted by some radioactive materials (**see topic 98**) • used in medicine to kill cancer cells and to trace blood flow • used to kill harmful bacteria on food and surgical instruments • large doses may damage human cells
	x-rays 	• pass through soft tissue but not bones or metals • used to kill cancer cells and to produce shadow images of bones • large doses may damage human cells
	ultraviolet	• causes tanning of the skin • large doses may cause skin cancer
medium wavelength 0.5×10^{-6} m	**violet** visible light **red**	• detected by the eye • used for vision and photography • used through optical fibres for viewing inside the human body and other inaccessible places
	infrared 	• radiated from warm and hot objects and causes heating • used in grills, toasters and radiant heaters • used in remote control devices, security cameras and communication
	microwaves	• some wavelengths absorbed by water used in cooking, but can damage living cells • longer wavelengths used in radar, mobile phones and satellite communication
long wavelengths 1 m–100 000 m low frequency 10^4 Hz	**radiowaves**	• broad range of wavelengths used in communication

The electromagnetic spectrum is a family of waves that all travel at the same speed in a vacuum.

These waves are called **electromagnetic waves**.

Test yourself

1 Suggest one reason why doctors prefer to use ultrasound rather than x-rays to image a baby in the womb.

2 Why should you take care not to stay in sunlight too long on a sunny day?

3 How can infrared cameras 'see' people and animals at night?

4 Why might people be concerned about the safety of mobile phones?

Waves

Check the facts

Modern communications use a broad spread of the electromagnetic spectrum to transmit information.

Early **optical fibres** used total internal reflection to transmit light. Doctors use fibres like this to see inside patients.

Modern fibres are so fine that infrared passes straight down the cable.

Telephone companies use cables of optical fibres to transmit telephone calls, computer signals and television programmes.

An optical fibre carries many more messages than a copper cable of similar thickness, and less energy is lost along the way.

Microwaves are used to transmit telephone calls across the country from transmitter to transmitter. Microwaves travel in straight lines but the Earth's curvature limits the distance between transmitters to about 40 km.

To get signals around the world microwaves carry the signals into space where an orbiting satellite picks up the signal and bounces it on its way. Television broadcasts are sent this way too. The dish on the outside of a house collects the signals from the satellite.

Radiowaves have been used to send information for a hundred years. The long wavelengths are ideally suited for sending signals across the country. The waves **diffract** around buildings to reach most places.

A recent revolution is the increasing use of digital signalling. A conventional telephone converts sound waves to a changing electrical signal whose pattern matches the original wave. This is called an **analogue signal**.

Waves

Modern telephone systems convert the analogue electrical signal to a **digital signal**. The digital signal consists of a stream of numbers that describes how the analogue signal changes. E-mail and faxes are sent by digital signals too.

Advantages of digital signals:

- they suffer less from interference
- they allow the optical fibre or radio wave to carry even more information, many television channels or lots of telephone conversations.

Test yourself

1 Give two advantages of using optical fibres rather than copper wire to transmit telephone information.

2 Give two advantages of using microwaves rather than cables to transmit long-distance telephone calls.

3 Give two advantages of using digital signals to transmit information.

h **4** What property of radio waves enables them to pass around tall buildings?

Waves

BBC GCSE Check and Test: Science

Check the facts

The Earth has a layered structure.

The thin outer part, called the **lithosphere**, is rigid and is about 70 km thick.

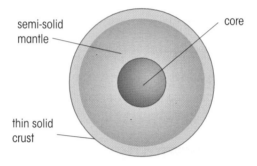

semi-solid mantle

core

thin solid crust

The lithosphere is broken into large plates that are moved by slow **convection currents** in the largely solid **mantle** beneath.

> **Where the plates move apart, molten rock rises and solidifies to form new plate material.**

> **Where the plates move together mountains may form by folding, volcanoes may erupt and earthquakes occur.**

The rock record gives us evidence to support these **plate tectonic** ideas.

- Africa and South America have closely matching coastlines and the rocks and the fossil records suggest that they were once close together.

- When new plate material forms under oceans, as the molten rock solidifies, it records the direction of the Earth's magnetic field. The magnetic patterns give us information about the way the plates have formed.

Test yourself

1 Two plates are moving apart under the Atlantic Ocean.

   a) What would you expect to see at the junction between the plates?

   b) What may happen as the convection currents move the plates apart?

2 What evidence is there that the plate tectonic theory is correct?

Waves

Check the facts

> **Earthquakes occur when moving tectonic plates stick and then move suddenly. This happens at the earthquake epicentre.**

The shock from large earthquakes shakes the ground surface and can destroy buildings. Some of the energy is carried through the Earth by waves called **seismic waves**.

Seismologists use information about the types of waves that are transmitted and how long they take to arrive at different 'listening stations' to learn more about the structure of the Earth.

Seismic primary (P) waves are the fastest. They are **longitudinal waves** that can travel through solids, liquids or gases and can pass right through the Earth.

Secondary (S) waves are slower, **transverse waves**. These waves only pass through solids. They stop at the core, showing that the outer core is liquid.

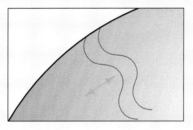

P waves are **refracted** at the junction between the mantle and the core. This means there are some parts of the Earth where P waves from a large earthquake do not arrive at all and other parts where they arrive late.

Test yourself

1 Give three differences between P waves and S waves.

2 Explain why there will be a significant time delay between the arrival of P waves and S waves at listening stations around the world. Where will the delay be longest?

Waves

BBC GCSE Check and Test: Science

Check the facts

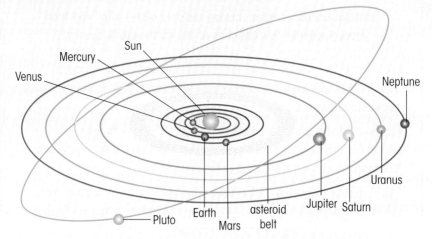

Sun, Mercury, Venus, Neptune, Uranus, Jupiter, Saturn, asteroid belt, Earth, Mars, Pluto

Earth and beyond

The Solar System consists of the Sun, nine planets, the asteroid belt and a number of comets.

All the planets except Pluto have orbits in the same plane.

The orbit of each of the planets is an ellipse. The orbit of Pluto is a more elongated ellipse and is at an angle to the plane of the other planets.

Between the four inner planets and the outer planets lies the asteroid belt, made up of dust and rocks.

All the bodies orbiting the Sun are held in their orbit by **gravity**.

The strength of the gravitational force depends on the mass of the body, the mass of the Sun and how close the body is to the Sun.

The time a planet takes to orbit the Sun is its year.

The further the planet is from the Sun, the weaker the pull of gravity. This means it moves more slowly and so its year is longer.

The Moon is a natural **satellite** of the Earth. Other planets have satellites too.

There are also many artificial satellites in orbit around the Earth. They too are held in orbit by gravity and the time taken to complete one orbit depends on their distance from the Earth.

Comets make very eccentric orbits of the Sun, sometimes coming in close and fast and at other times travelling a long way, far beyond Pluto.

www.bbc.co.uk/revision

Test yourself

1 The diagram shows the three innermost planets of the Solar System.

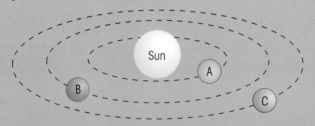

   a) Name the planet labelled B?
   b) Which planet has the shortest year, A, B or C?
   c) Draw on the diagram the path of a comet.
   d) Write an X on the comet's path where its speed is the greatest.

2 What is the name of the Earth's only natural satellite?

3 What force keeps this satellite in orbit around the Earth?

Earth and beyond

BBC GCSE Check and Test: Science

Earth and beyond

Check the facts

The Sun is just one star in the galaxy called the Milky Way.

You can see stars that are fairly close to the Earth as pinpoints of light. But most of the Milky Way appears as a faint band of light in the night sky.

Our galaxy is just one of many millions in the universe. Some galaxies appear as points of light in the night sky, others are so far away that they cannot be seen with the naked eye.

Since the universe began, many stars have been formed and have died. Stars are formed when **gravity** pulls together massive clouds of dust and gas in space. As the mass falls together it gets hot. If it gets hot enough for hydrogen nuclei to fuse together to make helium, a star is formed. The **fusion** process releases energy, keeping the core of the star hot.

The force of gravity holds the star together against the enormous pressures caused by the high temperatures. The Sun is at this stable period in its life.

As the hydrogen is used up in the fusion process, larger nuclei begin to form and the star may expand to become a **red giant**. When all the nuclear reactions are over, a small star (e.g. our Sun) may begin to contract under gravity. It becomes a **white dwarf** as it fades and cools.

With a larger, more massive star nuclear reactions may continue and the star will continue getting hotter and expanding until it explodes as a supernova. A **supernova** throws dust and gases into space, leaving a small dense neutron star, which shrinks to a **black hole**.

Observations suggest that all the galaxies in the universe are moving apart very quickly. Those further away seem to be moving faster. Evidence suggests the universe began with a **big bang**, which threw matter out in all directions.

Test yourself

1 How are stars formed?

2 What is the likely end to our star, the Sun?

3 Suggest what happens to the dust and gases thrown out by a supernova.

www.bbc.co.uk/revision

Check the facts

When you lift a weight, you do some **work**. If you lift a lot of weights, your arms will remind you that you are doing a lot of work.

You are transferring energy from your muscles to the weight.

When you push a broken-down car along the road you are doing work. You have to exert a **force** to overcome the friction within the car engine and wheels and between the wheels and the ground.

You measure work and energy in joules (J) and kilojoules (kJ).
1 kilojoule = 1000 joules

You can calculate the work done when a force moves something through a distance:

work done (J) = force (N) × distance (m)

Test yourself

1 A builder uses a force of 250 N to carry a hod of bricks up 5 metres. How much work does she do?

2 A weightlifter raises 120 kg through 1.5 metres.

a) What force does she need to use to lift 120 kg?
b) How much work does she do in lifting the load 1.5 metres?

3 A car needs a force of 2000 N to pull a caravan.

a) How much work is done by the car in moving the caravan 200 m?
b) Give your answer to 3a) in kilojoules.

BBC GCSE Check and Test: Science

Check the facts

A builder's mate who only carries one hod of bricks an hour up the ladder would not stay in the job very long. The rate of work is important too.

Rate of work or energy transfer is called power.

> **Q** How much food does the labourer need to eat to do the job?
>
> **A** Well, it is certainly more than the work done.

The labourer gets energy from the food she eats. Not all the energy from the food eaten is transferred to lifting loads.

Efficiency tells you how much of the energy input becomes useful output.

$$\text{energy efficiency} = \frac{\text{useful energy output}}{\text{total energy input}}$$

Test yourself

1 A stair-lift can lift a 800 N man 2.0 m in 10 seconds.
  a) How much work does the stair-lift do?
  b) What is the power of the stair-lift?
  c) Why would the stair-lift need more power than this?

2 An athlete in training weighs 60 kg. She does 100 step-ups in 3 minutes. Each step lifts her body 20 cm.
  a) What is her weight in newtons?
  b) How far does she step up altogether in 3 minutes?
  c) How much work does she do in 3 minutes?
  d) What is the athlete's power?

Check the facts

When an object is warmer than its surroundings, energy is transferred from the object to the colder surroundings.

This transfer often happens by **conduction**.

Metals	good conductors
Most non-metals	poor conductors

Poor conductors are used as **insulators**. Insulators are sometimes used to keep something hot and sometimes to keep something cold.

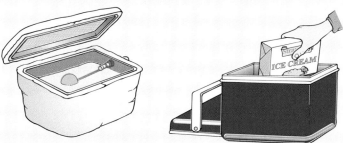

Test yourself

1 Look at the pictures and explain whether each part indicated by an arrow is a good insulator or conductor. Explain why it is used in that situation.

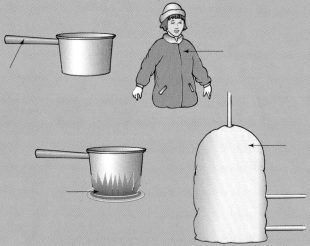

2 We spend a lot of money on energy to keep our houses warm.

a) Describe three ways in which energy is lost from our homes in winter.

b) How could we reduce these losses, and so reduce our energy bills?

Energy resources and transfer

BBC GCSE Check and Test: Science

Energy resources and transfer

Check the facts

When the builder carries the bricks up the ladder she is doing work. Energy is transferred from the food energy in her muscles to the bricks. The bricks store energy in the Earth's gravitational field. The bricks have gained **gravitational potential energy**.

Q What happens to that potential energy if the builder drops the bricks?

A The bricks fall to the ground, accelerating as they go. The moving bricks are said to have kinetic energy.

Q What happens to the kinetic energy of the bricks when they hit the ground?

A Some of the energy will break bonds within the bricks and the bricks will disintegrate; some of the energy is carried away by sound waves to the ears of the builder and some of the energy will shake the ground.

You can calculate the gain in gravitational potential energy by:

$$\text{potential energy (J)} = \text{mass (kg)} \times \text{gravitational field strength (N/kg)} \times \text{height lifted (m)}$$

$$PE = mgh$$

You can calculate the kinetic energy using the equation:

$$\text{kinetic energy (J)} = \tfrac{1}{2} \times \text{mass (kg)} \times \text{speed}^2 \text{ (m/s}^2)$$

$$KE = \tfrac{1}{2} mv^2$$

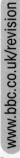

Test yourself

1 For each of these pictures:

a) say whether the object has kinetic energy and/or gravitational
   potential energy

b) explain where the energy came from to get the object to where
   it is now.

2 A student is filling shelves in a supermarket. Each can of beans weighs
500 g and has to be lifted 1.2 m on to the shelf. 200 cans need to be
transferred from the box to the shelf.

a) What is the mass of one can in kg?

b) What is the weight of one can in newtons?

c) How much work does the student do in lifting one can on to the shelf?

d) How much work is done in lifting 200 cans on to the shelf?

e) The student does the job in 3 minutes. What was the average power
   during this time?

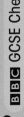

Energy resources and transfer

Check the facts

Most energy is supplied to our homes through the electricity supply, the National Grid.

Q Where does the energy come from to generate electricity?

A The biggest energy source for power stations is **fossil fuels**.

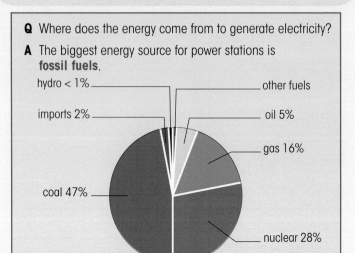

- hydro < 1%
- imports 2%
- coal 47%
- other fuels
- oil 5%
- gas 16%
- nuclear 28%

Fossil fuels:

- are burned in power stations to heat water to drive the turbines which turn the generators

- are also used to transport both people and goods around the country

- are a finite resource – one day they will run out.

Test yourself

1 A car burns petrol to drive the engine. What has happened to the energy in the petrol by the end of a car journey?

2 A coal-fired power station has an efficiency of 35%. What does an efficiency of 35% mean?

3 There are other ways of driving generators than using steam turbines. Give two ways and suggest advantages and disadvantages of each.

4 It would be more energy-efficient for people to use public transport to travel to work.
   a) Explain why this is so.
   b) Give one other way in which city life would be better if more people used public transport.
   c) Suggest a reason why more people do not use public transport.

Check the facts

Radiation	What is it?	How far can it travel in air?	What stops it?	What happens in a magnetic field?
alpha α	particles (positive helium) nuclei	a few centimetres	thin paper	small deflection
beta β	particles (negative electrons)	a few metres	thin aluminium	large deflection
gamma γ	electromagnetic radiation	several kilometres	thick lead	no deflection

Radioactive decay is a random process that takes place in the nuclei of some elements.

Nuclei are unstable and spontaneously emit radiation. Radiation ionises molecules in cells, which may damage or kill the cell. There are three kinds of radiation: **alpha** (α), **beta** (β) and **gamma** (γ).

The **nucleus of an atom** contains **protons** and **neutrons**. The protons are positively charged and the neutrons have no charge. Some nuclei are not stable due to too many neutrons. When alpha or beta particles are emitted, the proton and neutron numbers change. This is now a different element.

Radioactivity is all around you. Some rocks are naturally radioactive; radioactive particles called cosmic rays come from the Sun and elsewhere in our galaxy. Both these sources of radiation give rise to radioactive particles in the air you breathe. This radiation has always been there and is called **background radiation**. You must remember to take background radiation into account when making radioactivity measurements.

Test yourself

1 What property of alpha and beta particles causes them to be deflected when they pass through a magnetic field?

2 Which radiation could reach us from outer space? Explain your answer.

3 How many protons and neutrons are there in an alpha particle?

4 Why would it be more dangerous to have an open source of gamma radiation in the room than a source of alpha or beta radiation?

5 Why is beta radiation the best to measure paper thickness in a paper mill?

Radioactivity

BBC GCSE Check and Test: Science

Check the facts

Radioactive decay is a random process that makes the **nucleus** more stable.

You cannot predict when a particular nucleus will decay. However, you can say that after a certain amount of time half the nuclei in a sample will have decayed.

The time taken for half the nuclei to decay is called the half-life.

As the nuclei decay, there will be less of the material left to decay. Half of the remaining nuclei will decay in another half-life.

Example

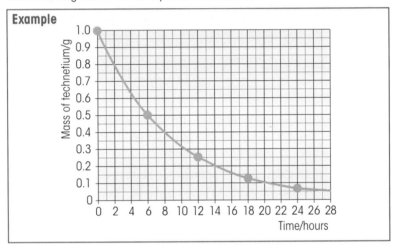

The graph above shows how a sample of technetium decays.

Technetium is used as a chemical tracer in hospitals.

The half-life of technetium is about six hours. Every six hours half the technetium decays, so the rate of decay decreases.

Test yourself

1 Look at the graph of technetium decay.

   a) How long does it take the mass to change from 0.8 g to 0.4 g?

   b) Does this agree with the statement that the half-life of technetium is six hours?

2 Uranium-235 is found in some igneous rocks. It decays to lead-207 with a half-life of 700 million years. Why is uranium-235 a good element to use for dating rocks?

Check the facts

Care must be taken when handling radioactive materials. People who work with ionising radiation must take particular care; the greater the dose, the greater the risk of damage.

> **There are ways of using ionising radiation to benefit people.**

Radiation damages cells. Careful application of radiation can be used to destroy cancerous cells, while leaving healthy cells unharmed.

The radiation may be applied from a source outside the body or from within the body.

Gamma radiation can be used in a similar way to x-rays to produce an image of the body. This is used in diagnosis.

The ability of radiation to penetrate a known distance through materials is used to measure the thickness of a variety of materials in manufacturing.

Radioactivity

Test yourself

1 In the picture, cobalt-60 is used as a source of gamma radiation to destroy cancerous cells. The source is directed at the tumour, but rotated in a circle and aimed at the body from different directions.

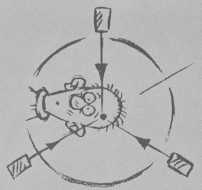

a) Explain why a gamma source is best for therapy from outside the body.

b) Suggest two reasons why the source is rotated around the body and not just aimed from one direction.

2 An isotope of iodine, iodine-131, is a beta-emitter. Explain why this is taken internally to treat cancer of the thyroid.

BBC GCSE Check and Test: Science

Chemical names and formulae

Acids

hydrochloric acid **HCl**
sulphuric acid **H_2SO_4**
nitric acid **HNO_3**
carbonic acid **H_2CO_3**

> **Remember**
> Acid + Base - Salt + Water
> Acid + Metal - Salt + Hydrogen
> Acid + Carbonate - Salt + Water + Carbon Dioxide

Bases

copper oxide **CuO**
lead oxide **PbO_2**
magnesium oxide **MgO**
calcium oxide **CaO**

> **Remember**
> Bases are oxides and
> hydroxides of metals

alkalis {
calcium hydroxide **$Ca(OH)_2$** - lime - water:
goes milky with carbon dioxide
sodium hydroxide **NaOH**
potassium hydroxide **KOH**
ammonium hydroxide **NH_4OH**
}

> **Remember**
> An alkali is a soluble base

Salts

sodium chloride **NaCl**
copper sulphate **$CuSO_4$**
sodium carbonate **Na_2CO_3**
calcium carbonate **$CaCO_3$** - limestone, marble chips
ammonium sulphate **$(NH_4)_2SO_4$** } nitrogenous
ammonium nitrate **NH_4NO_3** } fertilisers

Common Gases

oxygen **O_2**   hydrogen sulphide **H_2S**
ammonia **NH_3**   nitrogen **N_2**
hydrogen chloride **HCl**   carbon monoxide **CO**
chlorine **Cl_2**   hydrogen **H_2**
carbon dioxide **CO_2**   sulphur dioxide **SO_2**

Ores

haematite: iron (III) oxide, **Fe_2O_3**
copper pyrites: copper (I) sulphide, **Cu_2S**
bauxite: aluminium oxide **Al_2O_3**
zinc blende: zinc sulphide **ZnS**

Some organic compounds

methane **CH_4**   ethanoic acid   **CH_3COOH**
ethane **C_2H_6**   vinyl chloride (chloroethene) **C_2H_3Cl**
ethene **C_2H_4**   chloroethane   **C_2H_5Cl**
ethanol **C_2H_5OH**   aminoethane (ethylamine)   **$C_2H_5NH_2$**

Types of chemical reactions

Some types of reaction

Combustion: burning in air or oxygen,

e.g. $2H_2 + O_2 \rightarrow 2H_2O$

Thermal decomposition: breaking down a compound by heat,

e.g. $CuCO_3 \xrightarrow{\text{heat}} CuO + CO_2$

Neutralisation: reacting an acid and an alkali together to give a salt solution which has pH7 (neutral),

e.g. $HCl + NaOH \rightarrow NaCl + H_2O$

Displacement: when a more reactive metal takes the place of a less reactive metal or a more reactive halogen takes the place of a less reactive halogen,

e.g. $Mg + ZnSO_4 \rightarrow MgSO_4 + Zn$
$Cl_2 + 2KBr \rightarrow 2KCl + Br_2$

Redox: when oxidation and reduction take place together in one reaction,

e.g.
$$\overset{\displaystyle \overset{\text{reduction}}{\longmapsto}}{CuO + H_2 \longrightarrow Cu + H_2O} \underset{\text{oxidation}}{\longmapsto}$$

Polymerisation: when small, single molecules (monomers) join into long chains (polymers),

e.g. $n\,C_2H_4 \rightarrow (C_2H_4)n$

ethene   polythene

Electrolysis: passing electricity through a molten ionic compound or an ionic compound in solution,

e.g. $2NaCl \xrightarrow{\text{electricity}} 2Na + Cl_2$
molten

Reversible reaction: a reaction which can proceed in either direction,

e.g. $N_2 + 3H_2 \rightleftharpoons 2NH_3$

BBC GCSE Check and Test: Science

Electricity and magnetism

You should be able to use these relationships:

- voltage = current × resistance
  (volts)   (amps)   (ohms)

  $V = IR$

- electrical power = voltage × current
  (watts)   (volts)   (amps)

  $P = VI$

- charge   = current × time
  (coulombs)   (amps) (seconds)

- For a transformer:

$$\frac{\text{voltage across primary}}{\text{voltage across secondary}} = \frac{\text{number of turns in primary coil}}{\text{number of turns in secondary coils}}$$

You need to be able to use these relationships:

- power (watts) = $\dfrac{\text{work done or energy transferred (joules)}}{\text{time taken (seconds)}}$

- energy (kilowatt-hours) = power (kilowatts) × time (hours)

You should know these circuit symbols:

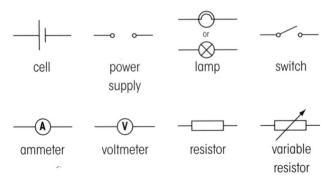

cell   power   lamp   switch
              supply

ammeter   voltmeter   resistor   variable
                                           resistor

Forces and motion

You should be able to use these relationships:

- average speed $=$ $\dfrac{\text{distance travelled (m)}}{\text{time taken (s)}}$
  (m/s)

- average speed $=$ $\dfrac{\text{change in velocity (m/s)}}{\text{time taken (s)}}$
  (m/s²)

- force $=$ mass $\times$ acceleration
  (newtons) (kilograms) (m/s²)
  $F = ma$

You need to be able to use the relationship:

- weight $=$ mass $\times$ gravitational
  (newtons) (kilograms) field strength
  $W = mg$ (N/kg)

h Waves

You should be able to use this relationship:

- wave speed $=$ frequency $\times$ wavelength
  (m/s) (hertz) (metres)
  $v = f\lambda$

Energy

You should know and be able to use this relationship:

- energy $=$ work $=$ force $\times$ distance
  transferred done (newtons) (metres)
  (joules)

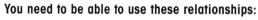

You need to be able to use these relationships:

- potential$=$ mass $\times$ gravitational $\times$ height
  energy (kg) field strength lifted
  (J) (N/kg) (m)

  $PE = mgh$

- kinetic $=$ $\frac{1}{2} \times$ mass $\times$ speed²
  energy (kilograms) (m/s)²
  (joules)
  $KE = \frac{1}{2}mv^2$

- energy efficiency $=$ $\dfrac{\text{useful energy output}}{\text{total energy input}}$

Answers

01 Cells
1 (a) Performs photosynthesis.
   (b) Controls all activities in the cell.
   (c) Controls entry/exit of substances.
2 Chloroplasts, cell wall, cell vacuole.
3 Red blood cell.

02 Cell division
1 (a) Mitosis.
   (b) Meiosis.
2 23.
3 Nucleus.
4 A = chromosome. B = cell membrane.

03 Respiration
1 Lactic Acid.
2 Oxygen.
3 Alcoholic drinks, beer, wine or bread.

04 Diffusion and osmosis
1 (a) Osmosis involves passage of water only, never solutes or solutions; osmosis happens across a semi-permeable membrane.
   (b) Water is more concentrated in soil solution than in the vacuole because cell sap contains more dissolved solutes than soil solution. Water passes from high concentration (high water potential) to low concentration (low water potential) through a semi-permeable membrane (cell membrane).
2 If salt solution is added to the soil, there is a lower concentration of water inside the cell than outside, so there is a net flow of water out of the roots so the plant dies from dehydration.
3 Water passing into kidney tubules or into guard cells of stomata in plants.

05 Breathing
1 In A, the diaphragm is flattened; in B the diaphragm is dome-shaped. In A the ribs have moved upwards; in B the ribs slope downwards.
2 (a) Decreases. (b) Increases.

06 Oxygen debt
1 Anaerobic.
2 (a) A: 95dm^3; B: 16dm^3.
   (b) The athletes need to repay the debt so they need to take in more oxygen than during norma activity.
3 Glucose $\rightarrow$ Lactic acid (+ Energy).

07 The heart
1 The left ventricle has to pump blood around the body but the right ventricle only has to pump blood to the lungs.
2 To stop back-flow of blood into atria.
3 (a) The pulse rate has increased during exercise so that more blood can be pumped to the muscles to supply them with glucose and oxygen. After the exercise the pulse rate gradually returns to normal.
   (b) The breathing rate would follow a similar pattern.
   (c) When the skin appears red, it means that its blood vessels have dilated (become wider) so that excess heat can be lost by radiation to keep the body temperature constant.

08 Enzymes
1 A biological catalyst.
2 (a) Liver.
   (b) Most froth is produced, therefore most enzyme and waste products, therefore cells are most active.
3 Temperature, pH.
4 No froth would be produced.
5 Average values will be more reliable, eliminating 'freak' results.

09 Insulin
1 Insulin regulates the blood-sugar level to 0.1 g glucose / 100 cm3 blood. It helps remove excess glucose from the blood by being involved in changing excess glucose to glycogen, which is stored in the liver, and increasing the rate that glucose is used in the body.
2 Controlling the diet so carbohydrate intake is strictly regulated.
3 (a) Person P.
   (b) These coincide with meal times.

10 Sex hormones
1 Testosterone.
2 Testes.
3 Puberty or adolescence.
4 Deepens voice; enlarges larynx; makes body more muscular; causes sperm production; increases muscle development; causes facial, pubic, armpit, and chest hair to increase.

11 Blood

1 Red blood cell.
2 (a) Plasma.
  (b) Red blood cell.
  (c) Plasma and red blood cell.
3 B has a nucleus and is not round or A does not have a nucleus and is round (or biconcave or disc-shaped).
4 Glucose or amino acids or hormones or water or minerals or vitamins
5 Carbon dioxide passing into blood or oxygen passing into cells or water passing in both directions.
6 White cells ingest microbes. They also produce antibodies and antitoxins.

12 Absorption of food

1 Small intestine (ileum).
2 The epithelium is very thin to allow for the passage of materials from the small intestine; the blood capillary allows for absorption and transport of digested nutrients except fats; the lacteal is for the transport of fats.

13 The digestive system

1 It increases the surface area for lipase to work.
2 It must be digested and made soluble.
3 (a) Stomach   (b) Mouth   (c) Colon
4 (a) Stomach.
  (b) Mouth or duodenum.
5 (a) 2.5.
  (b) B
  (c) A requires acid. B requires alkali. If they were together they would neutralise each other.

14 The eye

1 In bright light.
2 This would protect the retina from damage or allow vision in dim light.
3 Blinking protects the eye from damage by particles entering. Tear production: when your eyes 'water', special glands produce tears containing an antibacterial chemical to protect your eyes from infection.
4 Accommodation is the automatic process used by the eye to focus an image on the retina. To focus near objects, the ciliary muscles contract and the lens becomes more convex (thicker), making it of shorter focal length. To focus on distant objects, the ciliary muscles relax and the lens becomes less convex (thinner).

15 Reflex action

1 1 = receptor; 2 = sensory neurone; 3 = relay neurone; 4 = motor neurone; 5 = effector; 6 = grey matter.
2 Reflex actions are fast, automatic ways of protecting you from danger.
3 Stimuli.
4 Ears: vibrations in the air; eyes: light; nose and tongue: chemicals in solution; skin: changes in temperature, touch, pressure.

16 Kidneys and excretion

1 To reabsorb glucose and other useful substances.
2 Blood pressure caused by the heart.
3 (a) Protein and glucose.
  (b) Protein remains in the blood because the molecules are too big to go through the filter. Glucose has been reabsorbed into the blood capillaries of the tubules.
  (c) Filtration and reabsorption.
4 Filtration under pressure forces small molecules through the capillary wall and retains cells and large molecules.

17 Kidneys and regulation

1 8
2 When there is little water available to the animal, very little is absorbed into the blood stream. When blood contains little water it triggers the production of antidiuretic hormone from the pituitary gland in the brain. This circulates in the blood and causes the kidneys to reabsorb as much water as possible. The longer the tubule, the more surface area it has to do this.
3 The desert rat needs to conserve as much as possible.

18 Temperature regulation

1 1: hair; 2: sweat pore; 3: sweat gland.
2 (a) Diameter becomes smaller.
  (b) Diameter becomes larger.
3 Sweat is produced; hairs lie flat on the surface.
4 Heat lost by latent heat of evaporation.

Answers

19 Photosynthesis

1 (a) Iodine.
  (b) Turns black.
2 Plants use carbon dioxide, produced by the fish, for photosynthesis which provide the fish with oxygen. The plants also provide food.
3 The conversion of light energy to chemical energy in food made by plants from carbon dioxide and water using chlorophyll.
4 Photosynthesis produces oxygen which reacts with iron to produce rust.

20 Transpiration

1 Stomata.
2 Transpiration.
3 (a) A: 3g, B: 0.5g, C: 0g.
  (b) The lower.

21 Plant hormones

1 The seedlings in A would be strong and upright with green leaves. The seedlings in B would be long and weak with small yellow leaves well-spaced on the stem. The seedlings in C would have grown towards the light.
2 Gravity; roots grow downwards, stems grow in the opposite direction.
3 Hormones (auxins).
4 It causes stems and leaves to gow towards light for photosynthesis.

22 Natural selection

1 (c)
2 Industrial pollution altered the moths' environment. Dark-coloured forms in the population were camouflaged from birds and so had a selective advantage and survived to breed. They were better adapted to the new environmental conditions. Light-coloured moths were at a disadvantage and were reduced in numbers.

23 Mutation

1 (a)
2 It was less well camouflaged so more easily seen by the birds that prey on it.
3 The black form of snail would be at an advantage because it would now be difficult to see against the blackened background so its numbers would increase.
4 The radioactive fallout increased the mutation rate. A gene mutation resulted in a new form. The brown form (well-camouflaged against the dark background) survived to breed and, as it was well-adapted to the environment, its numbers increased.

24 Gender determination

1 A = nucleus; B = chromosome.
2 (a) A = XX; B = XY.
  (b) A = female; B = male.

25 Genetic crosses

1 Chromosomes.
2 (a) bb.   (b) Bb, BB.
3 (a) Bb and Bb.   (b) 50%.

26 Inherited diseases

1 A disorder which can be inherited because it is controlled by one or more mutated genes.
2 Mucus blocks the bronchioles so air cannot pass in and out.
3 Bacteria trapped in the mucus are killed by antibiotics.
4 (a) (i) Nn (ii) Nn (iii) nn.
  (b) NN or Nn.

27 DNA (deoxyribonucleic acid)

1 (a) Double helix.
  (b) T with A and A with T.
2 Enzymes.

28 Genetic engineering

1 1 = (b); 2 = (a); 3 = (c).
2 Enzymes.
3 The production of large numbers of genetically identical cells.

29 Food chains

1 (a) The oak tree.
  (b) Bark beetle or caterpillar or mouse or squirrel or earthworm.
  (c) Hawk or owl or blackbird.
2 Bark → beetle → blackbird → hawk.
3 (a) Mice would increase because there are fewer owls to eat them.
  (b) Squirrels would decrease because there would be more competition for their food from mice.

30 Concentration through food chains

1 Some of the insecticide has reached the pond by being washed in by rain. Some has been taken into the plants

Answers

in the pond. When animals in the food chain feed on each other, the concentration of the insecticide builds up and eventually reaches a toxic level in the fish.

31 Food webs
1 Only plants can make food by photosynthesis.
2 Energy flow.
3 There would be a decrease in foxes and possibly an increase in animals that eat grass due to less competition.

32 Food pyramids
1 The diagram should be a triangle with the following levels, starting at the base and moving upwards: plants; snails and worms; insects and leeches; small fish; large fish.
2 Large fish.

33 The carbon cycle
1 = Respiration by microbes.
2 = Burning of coal and oil.
3 = Photosynthesis.
4 = Feeding.
5 = Decay.

34 The nitrogen cycle
1 Protein.
2 Bacteria and fungi.
3 1, 2 and 5.

35 Atomic structure
1

Atom	Sodium	Aluminium	Fluorine
number of protons	11	13	9
number of neutrons	12	14	8
number of electrons	11	13	9
atomic number	11	13	9
mass number	23	27	17

2 (a) 7p, 7n, 7e. (b) 5p, 6n, 5e.
 (c) 53p, 74n, 53e. (d) 15p, 16n, 15e.
 (e) 26p, 30n, 26e.
3 Because all atoms contain an equal number of positive protons and negative electrons.
4 The circulating negative electrons are held by attraction to the positive protons in the nucleus.
5 Each has 8 protons and 8 electrons. The different isotopes have 8, 9 or 10 neutrons respectively.

36 Electrons in atoms
1 The arrangement of electrons in the shells or energy levels of an atom.

2 (a) 2.4 (b) 2.6
 (c) 2.8.7 (d) 2.8.8

3 (a) 11 (b) 23
 (c) 11 (d) 12
 (e) 2.8.1

4

5 Five electrons in the outer shell.
6 (a) 2.8.8.1
 (b) 2.8.8.2
 (c) 2.8.9.2

37 Organic chemistry
1 The study of carbon compounds.
2 A compound containing only carbon and hydrogen.
3 The ability to use covalent bonding to form long chains.
4 (a) A compound containing only single bonds.
 (b) A compound containing only double bonds.
5 (a) CH_3OH (b) C_3H_7Cl (c) CH_3NH_2

38 Covalent bonding
1 A shared pair of electrons joining two atoms together. One electron from each atom makes up the pair.
2 A discrete particle made up of two or more atoms joined to each other by covalent bonds.
3 The forces between discrete, covalent molecules are very small and therefore the molecules are easy to separate from each other by heat energy. Hence covalent compounds have low melting and boiling points.
 Water (H_2O)

4 (a)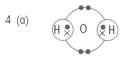

 (b) Ammonia (NH_3)

Answers

BBC GCSE Check and Test: Science

139

(c) Chlorine (Cl_2)

5 Giant molecules have large numbers of atoms joined into a continuous structure by covalent bonds. The heat energy required to separate these is extremely high and hence melting points also high.

6 A bond consisting of two shared pairs of electrons. Each pair has one electron from each atom.

7 Ethene C_2H_4

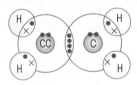

39 Ionic bonding

1 An atomic particle which has an electric charge due to the loss or gain of one or more electrons.

2 An ion with a single positive charge. The number of positive protons exceeds the number of negative electrons by one.

3 (a) K^+ (b) Ca^{2+} (c) O^{2-} (d) Mg^{2+} (e) Br^-

4 (a)

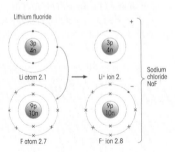

Lithium fluoride

Li atom 2.1 → Li⁺ ion 2.

F atom 2.7 F⁻ ion 2.8

Sodium chloride NaF

(b)

Calcium oxide

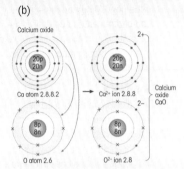

Ca atom 2.8.8.2 → Ca^{2+} ion 2.8.8

Calcium oxide CaO

O atom 2.6 O^{2-} ion 2.8

5 (a) Both have an electronic configuration of 2.8 but they have different numbers of protons and hence different charges. Sodium has 11 protons so its ion is unipositive; the magnesium ion has 12 protons and so has two positive charges.

(b) Both have the same electronic configuration of 2.8 but they have different numbers of protons and hence different charges. The magnesium ion has 12 protons and so has two positive charges; the oxide ion has 8 protons and so has two negative charges.

40 Reactivity and the extraction of metals

1 A list of metals arranged in order of reactivity, the most reactive at the top.

2 (a) Two of potassium, sodium, calcium, magnesium.

(b) Two of lead, copper, mercury, silver, gold.

3 (a) zinc + lead nitrate → zinc nitrate + lead

(b) lead + copper sulphate → lead sulphate + copper

(c) no reaction

(d) copper + silver nitrate → copper nitrate + silver

4 Lithium is a very reactive metal with compounds too stable to be reduced chemically.

5 Reactive metals have stable compounds which are difficult to reduce; unreactive metals have less stable compounds which are easier to reduce.

41 Extraction by reduction

1 A rock from which metals are obtained.

2 Four of zinc, iron, lead, copper, mercury.

3 Zinc blende (zinc sulphide).
The ore is roasted in air and the oxide obtained is reduced to zinc by heating with coke (carbon).
$2ZnS (s) + 3O^2 (g) \rightarrow 2ZnO (s) + 2SO2 (g)$
$2ZnO (s) + C (s) \rightarrow 2Zn (s) + CO^2 (g)$

4 $2PbO (s) + C (s) \rightarrow 2Pb (s) + CO^2 (g)$
lead oxide + carbon $\rightarrow$ lead + carbon dioxide

42 Extraction by electrolysis

1 In molten sodium chloride the ions are free to move from place to place; in solid sodium chloride the ions are fixed in place.

2 Sodium ion, Na^+; chloride ion, Cl^-.

3 The ions present are Na^+ and Cl^-. The Na+ ions are attracted to the negative cathode where they gain electrons to become sodium atoms:
$2Na^+ + 2e^- \rightarrow 2Na (s)$
The chloride ions are attracted to the positive anode where they give up electrons to form chlorine molecules:
$2Cl^- - 2e^- \rightarrow Cl_2 (g)$
Overall the reaction is:
$2NaCl (l) \rightarrow 2Na (s) + Cl_2 (g)$

4 Blister copper is the impure copper extracted from the ore copper pyrites by heating the ore in air. The copper pyrites is reduced to copper.
$Cu_2S (s) + O_2 (g) \rightarrow 2Cu (s) + SO_2 (g)$

5 (a) The ions present are K^+ and Cl^-. The electrolysis proceeds exactly as in question 3, substituting K^+ for Na^+ and K for Na in the equations.
(b) The ions present are Al^{3+} and O^{2-}. At the anode the oxide ions each give up two electrons to form oxygen molecules:
$2O^{2-} - 4e^- \rightarrow O^2$
At the cathode the aluminium ions each gain three electrons to form aluminium.
$Al^{3+} + 3e^- \rightarrow Al$

The overall reaction is:
$2Al_2O_3 (l) \rightarrow 4Al (s) + 3O_2 (g)$

6 The forces between the multi-charged Al^{3+} and O^{2-} ions of the aluminium oxide are approximately three times greater than the forces between the uni-charged Na^+ and Cl^- ions of the sodium chloride.

43 Fractional distillation

1 Because it has been formed over millions of years from plant and animal remains.

2 Heating crude oil to separate it into its different components by means of their different boiling points.

3 Any three of the fractions from the table in the text, together with the appropriate information.

4 (a) $CH_4 + 2O_2 \rightarrow 2H_2O + CO_2$
(b) $2C_4H_{10} + 13O_2 \rightarrow 10H_2O + 8CO_2$
(c) $2C_{10}H_{22} + 31O_2 \rightarrow 22H_2O + 20CO_2$

44 Polymerisation

1 Breaking long hydrocarbons down into smaller molecules using high temperatures and, usually, a catalyst.

2 Because they are unsaturated hydrocarbons. The double bond can be broken and the carbon atoms can join together to form long chains.

3 The making of polymers (long chain molecules of thousands of carbon atoms) from monomers (small single molecules with a double bond). The monomers join together when heated under pressure in the presence of a catalyst. An example is polythene.

4
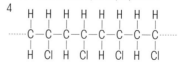

(The number of C atoms shown in the section is not important but each alternate C atom should have a Cl atom attached.)

Answers

45 Products from air

1 Nitrogen, oxygen and carbon dioxide.
2 78% nitrogen, 21% oxygen.
3 Ammonia.
4 The air.
5 N_2 (g) + $3H_2$ (g) $\xrightleftharpoons[\substack{500-550°C \\ Fe\ catalyst}]{250\ atmospheres}$ $2NH_3$ (g) + heat
6 Artificial fertiliser containing nitrogen.
7 $2NH_3$ (g) + H_2SO_4 (aq) $\rightarrow$ $(NH_4)_2SO_4$ (aq)
   NH_3 (g) + HNO_3 (aq) $\rightarrow$ NH_4NO_3 (aq)
8 Nitrogen is required to make proteins for healthy growth.
9 By taking nitrogen compounds from soil and converting them to protein.
10 Fertilisers are needed to replace the nutrients in soil as they are depleted by continuous use of the soil.
11 Fertilisers produce high yields of healthy crops and do this quickly.

46 The atmosphere and the oceans

1 When plant life formed it began to photosynthesise, using the carbon dioxide in the atmosphere and producing oxygen.
2 Oxygen levels increased steadily as more plants appeared on the Earth and produced oxygen by photosynthesis. When animal life appeared the oxygen was used for respiration and levels fell. Eventually a balance was reached between the production of oxygen by photosynthesis and its use in respiration so that the level remained stable.
3 The seas were at first pure, condensed water but then minerals from the Earth's crust and gases from the atmosphere dissolved in the water.
4 As forests are cleared there are fewer plants to use carbon dioxide in photosynthesis. Thus carbon dioxide levels increase and add to the greenhouse effect.

47 Natural cycles: the carbon cycle

1 Materials are continually produced and used up but a balance is maintained by recycling.
2 Three of, for example, carbon, nitrogen, water, rock.
3 Atmospheric carbon dioxide is taken in by plants during photosynthesis. Animals eat these plants. When plants and animals die the carbon returns to the soil via the decomposed remains.
4 Carbon is returned to the atmosphere by the respiration of plants and animals, the bacterial decay of plant and animal remains and the burning of fossil fuels. (Only two of these required by the question.)
5 Burning fossil fuels puts CO2 into the atmosphere. This is heavy and remains in the atmosphere.
   It then traps heat in and adds to the Greenhouse Effect.

48 Rocks

1 The first rocks on the Earth were formed by the cooling and solidification of molten rock (magma). This always produces igneous rock and not other types.
2 The removal of rock fragments by the impact of wind, water, rocks or animals, including humans.
3 Rock fragments, called sediment, are removed by erosion. Sediment is deposited in quieter conditions. Over millions of years the layers of sediment can build up and the lower, older layers are compacted and cemented together into sedimentary rocks.
4 The study of how sediments are formed, how volcanoes erupt and the effects of earthquakes today; the observation of rock features; the study of shock waves travelling through the Earth after an earthquake.
5 Dead plants and animals are trapped in the layers of sedimentary rocks. The fossils in the lower layers will be older than those in the more recently-deposited upper layers.

49 Balanced chemical equations

1 (a) $Zn + 2HCl \rightarrow ZnCl_2 + H_2$
  (b) $C + CO_2 \rightarrow 2CO$
  (c) $2H_2 + O_2 \rightarrow 2H_2O$
  (d) $2Al + Fe_2O_3 \rightarrow Al_2O_3 + 2Fe$
  (e) $2KOH + H_2SO_4 \rightarrow K_2SO_4 + 2H_2O$
  (f) $ZnSO_4 + 2NaOH \rightarrow Zn(OH)_2 + Na_2SO_4$
  (g) $2Pb(NO_3)\,2 \rightarrow 2PbO + 4NO_2 + O_2$
2 (a) $CuO + H_2 \rightarrow Cu + H_2O$
  (b) $2Na + 2H_2O \rightarrow 2NaOH + H_2$
  (c) $N_2 + 3H_2 \rightleftharpoons 2NH_3$

(d) $ZnCO_3 \rightarrow ZnO + CO_2$

(e) $2NaOH + MgCl_2 \rightarrow Mg(OH)_2 + 2NaCl$

50 Reacting masses

1　5.6g.

2　8g of oxygen are required; 9g of water are produced.

3　6.2g.

4　0.46g.

51 Determining formulae

1　$4 \div 1 = 4$ moles of hydrogen react with $32 \div 16 = 2$ moles of oxygen. The ratio is 2:1 so the formula of water is H_2O.

2　$2 \div 1 = 2$ moles of hydrogen react with $32 \div 32 = 1$ mole of sulphur. The ratio is 2:1 so the formula of hydrogen sulphide is H_2S.

3　Mass of chlorine $= 11.7 - 4.6g = 7.1g$. $4.6 \div 23 = 0.2$ moles sodium react with $7.1 \div 35.5 = 0.2$ moles chlorine. The ratio is 1:1 so the formula of sodium chloride is NaCl.

4　Mass of oxygen $= 4 - 3.2g = 0.8g$. $3.2 \div 64 = 0.05$ moles of copper react with $0.8 \div 16 = 0.05$ moles of oxygen. The ratio is 1:1 so the formula of copper oxide is CuO.

52 Introducing the periodic table

1　Table containing all the elements listed in order of atomic number, starting with hydrogen, atomic number 1.

2　A vertical column of elements having the same number of electrons in the outer shell. The group number is the same as the number of electrons in the outer shell.

3　Elements in a group have the same number of electrons in the outer shell and have similar chemical properties.

4　A horizontal row of elements with the same configuration of electrons in their inner shell(s) but with increasing numbers of electrons in the outermost shell as you move from left to right across the period.

5　Elements in a period have the same configuration of electrons in their inner shell(s).

6　The transition metals are those elements that fit in the periodic table between group II and group III.

53 Properties of elements

1　(a) Any two elements in group I, other than sodium.

(b) Any two elements in group II, other than calcium.

(c) Any two elements in group VI, other than sulphur.

(d) Any two elements in group VII, other than fluorine.

2　(a) The bottom element in group I.

(b) The top element in group VII.

(c) Period 3, sodium to argon.

(d) Group VI.

3　(a) Three of A, D, E, F; D is the most metallic.

(b) B and C; B is the most non-metallic.

(c) (i) D_2B　(ii) AB

(d) They are transition metals.

(e) No; they are both metals and metals do not form compounds with each other.

54 Noble gases

1　The atoms get heavier and so the inter-atomic forces become greater.

2　Because they do not undergo any chemical reactions as they already have complete outer electron shells.

3　The atoms existing singly. Atoms of the noble gases have complete outer shells and hence don't join to each other remaining as individual atoms.

4　It is lighter than air and non-flammable.

5　Its inertness prevents the filament from burning away.

55 Alkali metals

1　They all have a single electron in the outer shell.

2　The one outer electron is easier to lose as it gets further away from the positive nucleus and is, therefore, less strongly held.

3　(a) KCl

(b) Na_2O

(c) LiOH

4　(a) $2Na + Br_2 \rightarrow 2NaBr$ sodium bromide

(b) $4K + O_2 \rightarrow 2K_2O$ potassium oxide

(c) $2Na + 2H_2O \rightarrow 2NaOH + H_2$ sodium hydroxide and hydrogen

Answers

BBC GCSE Check and Test: Science

Answers

56 Alkali metal compounds

1 There is no reaction. Sodium is a very reactive metal and its compounds are stable to heat.

2 Potassium is a very reactive metal and its compounds are very stable. Electrolysis is therefore necessary. Molten potassium chloride is the electrolyte. Potassium is deposited at the anode and chlorine gas given off at the cathode.
$2KCl \ (l) \rightarrow 2K \ (s) + Cl_2 \ (g)$

3 (a) sodium carbonate
(b) sodium hydroxide
(c) sodium hydroxide
(d) sodium chloride
(e) sodium chloride
(f) sodium hydroxide
(g) sodium chloride
(h) sodium chloride

4 (a) $2K^+; O^{2-}$ (b) $Li^+; OH^-$
(c) $2Na^+; CO_3{}^{2-}$ (d) $2K^+; SO4^{2-}$
(e) $Na^+; NO^{3-}$ (f) $K^+; Br^-$

57 Halogens

1 (a) Dark brown or black.
(b) Solid.
(c) About 250°C.

2 (a) $2Na + I_2 \rightarrow 2NaI$ sodium iodide
(b) $Br_2 + H_2 \rightarrow 2HBr$ hydrogen bromide

3 Chlorine is reacted with hydrogen to form hydrogen chloride gas:
$Cl_2 \ (g) + H_2 \ (g) \rightarrow 2HCl \ (g)$
The hydrogen chloride gas is then dissolved in water to form hydrochloric acid:
$HCl \ (g) + H_2O \rightarrow HCl \ (aq)$

4 Iodine: between 90°C and 130°C.
Astatine: between 150°C and 200°C.

58 Halogen compounds

1 (a) $Cl_2 + 2NaBr \rightarrow 2NaCl + Br_2$
(b) No reaction.
(c) $Br_2 + 2NaI \rightarrow 2NaBr + I_2$
(d) No reaction.

2 (a) $Ca^{2+}; 2Cl^-$ (b) $Na^+; I^-$
(c) $Mg^{2+}; 2Br^-$ (d) $Li^+; Cl^-$

3 (a)

(b)

(c)

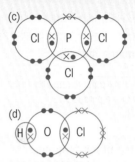

(d)

59 Transition metals

1 (a) The spaces in the incomplete shell allows electrons to move.
(b) The strong inter-atomic forces mean that high energy levels are required for melting to occur.
(c) The same number of electron shells are in use across the series.
(d) They all have similar electronic configurations, i.e. two electrons in the outermost (fourth) shell and an incomplete third shell (except zinc).
(e) They all lose electrons to form positive ions during reaction.

2 Zinc has complete inner shells as the non-transition metals do.

3 Zinc has complete inner shells of electrons so inter-atomic forces are lower in zinc than other transition metals. Hence the lower melting point.

60 Oxidation

1 Gain of oxygen or the loss of hydrogen.

2 A provider of oxygen or a remover of hydrogen.

3 (a) Oxidised: carbon (C); oxidising agent: zinc oxide (ZnO)
(b) Oxidised: carbon monoxide (CO); oxidising agent: iron oxide (Fe_2O_3)
(c) Oxidised: sulphur (S); oxidising agent: oxygen (O_2)
(d) Oxidised: hydrogen bromide (HBr); oxidising agent: chlorine (Cl_2)
(e) Oxidised: methane (CH_4); oxidising agent: chlorine (Cl_2).

4 (a) Sodium gains O_2 / loses electrons:
$Na - e^- \rightarrow Na^+$
(b) The calcium loses electrons:
$Ca - 2e^- \rightarrow Ca^{2+}$
(c) The sodium loses electrons:
$Na - e^- \rightarrow Na^+$
(d) The iron loses electrons:
$Fe - 2e^- \rightarrow Fe^{2+}$

61 Reduction and redox reactions

1 Loss of oxygen, gain of hydrogen or gain of electrons.

2 (a) aluminium (Al)
(b) iron oxide (Fe_2O_3)
(c) iron oxide (Fe_2O_3)
(d) aluminium (Al)

3 A reaction in which oxidation and reduction occur together.

4 Bromide ions (Br^-) are oxidised and chlorine molecule (Cl_2) is reduced.
$Cl_2 + 2e^- \rightarrow 2Cl^-$ $2Br^- - 2e^- \rightarrow Br_2$

5 When calcium burns in air, calcium oxide is formed.
$2Ca\ (s) + O_2\ (g) \rightarrow 2CaO\ (s)$
The calcium atoms lose 2 electrons each and thus calcium is oxidised.
$2Ca - 4e^- \rightarrow 2Ca^{2+}$ oxidation
The atoms in the oxygen molecule gain 2 electrons each and thus oxygen is reduced.
$O_2 + 4e^- \rightarrow 2O^{2-}$ reduction

62 Neutralisation

1 (a) A solution with pH lower than 7.
(b) A solution with pH greater than 7.

2 The reaction between an acid and an alkali. The product is neutral (pH = 7).

3 (a) $H_2SO_4 + 2KOH \rightarrow K_2SO_4 + 2H_2O$
(b) $H^+ + OH^- \rightarrow H_2O$

4 (a) $HCl + KOH \rightarrow KCl + H_2O$
(b) $H^+ + OH^- \rightarrow H_2O$

5 Dilute sulphuric acid conducts electricity well and so must contain many ions. Concentrated sulphuric acid is a poor conductor and so must contain few ions. The ionisation of sulphuric acid increases with dilution.

63 Thermal decomposition

1 The breaking down of a compound.

2 Breaking down of a compound by heat.

3 $MgCO_3 \rightarrow MgO + CO_2$
Magnesium oxide and carbon dioxide.

4 Sodium is a very reactive metal and so its compounds are stable to heat.

5 (a) Potassium is a reactive metal.
(b) By electrolysis: $2KCl \rightarrow 2K + Cl_2$

64 Enzymes

1 Enzymes are proteins found in the human body.

2 They catalyse the chemical reactions in the body.

3 They work by fitting into the reactant molecule like a jigsaw piece. Each enzyme catalyses one specific reaction.

4 Two of, for example, amylase, lysozyme, protease, pysozyme.

5 A biological washing powder works by chemical reactions similar to those occurring in the body. It contains enzymes called proteases which break down the proteins in the substances which stain clothes, such as oil and blood.

65 Patterns and predictions

1 (a) zinc + oxygen $\rightarrow$ zinc oxide
$2Zn + O_2 \rightarrow 2ZnO$
(b) copper oxide + hydrogen $\rightarrow$ copper + water
$CuO + H_2 \rightarrow Cu + H_2O$

2 (a) 2.6
(b) Group VI.
(c) Non-metal.
(d) Yes; Y^{2-}.
(e) Yes; covalent; two non-metals always form covalent compounds.

3 (a) magnesium + zinc sulphate $\rightarrow$ magnesium sulphate + zinc
(b) No reaction.
(c) zinc + copper sulphate $\rightarrow$ zinc sulphate + copper
(d) No reaction.

66 Rates of reaction

1 (a) For example: burning, precipitation, acids on carbonates.
(b) For example: cooking, decomposition (rotting) of food.

2 A collision between particles that have enough energy to cause reaction (activation energy) rather than bounce away from each other.

3 Inhibitors increase the activation energy needed for a fruitful collision.

67 Energy transfers in chemical reactions

1 (a) Methane and oxygen.
(b)

(c) DH is negative because the change in heat content is a downwards one, i.e. a negative one.

2 (a) 1 N—N bond and 3 H—H bonds.
  (b) 6 N—H bonds.
  (c) If DH is negative the reaction is exothermic. Hence the energy contained in the six N—H bonds is lower than the energy in the one N—N and three H—H bonds.
3 (a) DH = 436 + 224 + 2(–366) = –72 kJ/mole
  (b) Exothermic.

68 The Haber process

1 A reaction in which both forward and backward reactions take place simultaneously.
2 The point at which forward and backward reactions take place at the same rate.
3 The amounts of reactants and products present at equilibrium.
4 (a) The system will try to absorb the increased heat and, as the reaction is exothermic, the position of equilibrium will move towards the left.
  (b) Increasing container size allows the system to expand and hence move to the side with more molecules. The position of equilibrium moves towards the left.
  (c) No effect on the position of equilibrium.
  (d) It moves from left to right to replace the removed ammonia.
  (e) It moves from right to left to replace the removed nitrogen.

69 Electric current and voltage

1

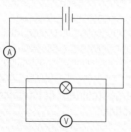

2 A: 0.2A; B: 0.5A.
3 (a) 0.5A.
  (b) 6V.

70 Resistance

1 voltage (volts) = current (amps) x resistance (Ω).
2 10 V.

3 (a)

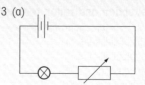

  (b) When the current in the circuit increases, more charge per second passes through the lamp. More energy per second is delivered by the current so the lamp glows more brightly.
4 48 Ω.

71 Components in circuits

1 As the current in the lamp increases, more energy is delivered to the lamp, so the temperature increases and so the resistance increases.
2 A diode only allows current to flow in one direction. Between -5 V and 0 V the voltage is negative and no current flows. As the voltage across the diode increases from 0 V to +5 V the current increases.
3 (a) As the light shining on an LDR gets brighter the resistance of the LDR decreases.
  (b) As the LDR resistance decreases, more current can flow in the circuit.

72 Electrical power and energy

1 (a) 36 W   (b) 10 800 J   (c) 4 Ω.
2 (a) 2000 W (b) 120 000 J (c) 8.7 A.

73 Electricity at home

1 0.25 kW.
2 (a) 6 kWh (b) 48 pence.
3 A fuse is designed to melt when the current in the circuit becomes too large. The fuse melts and breaks the circuit before other wires in the circuit overheat and cause a fire.
4 The earth wire is normally to the metal casing of an appliance to prevent the user getting a shock. Double insulated appliances do not have metal exposed to the user.
5 (a) 10 A.
  (b) 13 A. The other fuses would melt when the normal operating current passes through the circuit.

74 Electric charge

1 (a) Negative.
  (b) Positive.

(c)

The balloons have the same charge so will repel each other and move apart.

2 A jumper brushing against hair will transfer electrons from the jumper to the hair. The electrons make the hair negatively charged, so the individual hairs will repel each other, all trying to get as far apart as possible.

3 (a) 900 C   (b) 10 800 J.
  (c) 12 J   (d) 12 V.

75 Electric charge – good and bad

1 Walking across a carpet transfers charge from the carpet to your body. When you touch a door handle (a good conductor) some of the charge crosses from your hand to the handle; the current is felt as an electric shock.

2 The television screen becomes charged by the stream of electrons which cause the picture to form. The charge on the screen attracts dust particles.

3 The charged balloon attracts opposite charges in the wall, causing the two to stick together.

76 Electric motors

1 To increase the force on the wires and make the motor spin faster you can increase the current; have more turns on the coil or use stronger magnets. To make the force move the wire in the opposite direction you can reverse the current or the magnetic field.

2

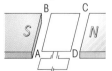

When the current is from A to B in one side of the coil it is from C to D in the other side of the coil. So AB moves up whilst CD moves down. When the coil is vertical there are no contacts so there is no current and the coil keeps turning. When side AB reaches the right-hand side the current is in the opposite direction in the magnetic field so the wire moves down, CD moves up and the coil continues to spin.

77 Electromagnetic induction

1 (a) The needle remains at zero (no induced voltage).
   (b) The needle flicks to the left (induced voltage in the opposite direction).
   (c) The needle flicks to the left (induced voltage in the opposite direction).
   (d) The needle flicks to the right.
   (e) The needle flicks to the right.

2 A voltage can only be induced in the secondary coil when there is a changing magnetic field in the iron core. The changing current in the primary coil produces the changing magnetic field. A direct current would produce a steady magnetic field and so no induced voltage.

3 10 V.

78 From power station to customer

1 The spinning magnet provides a magnetic field which passes through the coil. The movement of the magnet makes a constantly changing magnetic field through the coils.

2 Transformers need an alternating current to produce the changing magnetic field required to induce a voltage in the secondary coil. This is achieved by generating alternating current which then results in an a.c. output from the secondary coil.

3 Fossil fuels are a limited resource which will eventually be used up; fossil fuels are also used to make materials not easily made in other ways; burning fossil fuels increases air pollution; burning fossil fuels increases the carbon dioxide in the atmosphere, which contributes to global warming.

4 Not all the energy from the coal will heat the boiler – some transferred to the surroundings. Some energy from the hot pipes warms the atmosphere. Energy is lost to the surroundings

Answers

from the cooling towers. Energy is lost because the transmission cables become warm as the energy passes through them. Energy is lost in the transformers – they become warm and sometimes 'hum'.

5 (a) 8000 A (b) 500 A.

79 Distance and speed

1 25 m/s.

2 (a) 13.3 m/s.
(b) The cyclist was stationary.
(c) 10 m/s.
(d) The cyclist turned round and went back towards the origin at 10 m/s.

80 Acceleration

1 5 m/s^2

2 During the first 10 s the bus accelerates from 0 m/s^2 to 10 m/s^2. Between 10 s and 30 s it travels at a steady speed of 10 m/s. From 30 s to 40 s it accelerates from 10 m/s to 15 m/s and then travels at a steady speed of 15 m/s for 10 s. It slows down from 15 m/s to 5 m/s in 10 s.

3 8 m/s^2.

4 20 m/s.

81 Forces and motion

1 Parachutist: forces balanced so falling at a steady speed
Cyclist: force backwards greater so decelerating
Car: forward force greater so accelerating

2 (a) 2 m/s^2 (b) 3000 N.

3 40 N.

4 36 000 N

82 Stopping a car

1 15 m.

2 The thinking distance would be longer because the driver would take longer to realise he needs to brake and would therefore travel further.

3 79 m.

4 A wet road would reduce friction so the braking distance would be longer and the overall stopping distance would be longer.

5 The stopping force would be greater as the stopping time would be shorter so the deceleration would be greater.

6 The tyres would make the stopping distance and stopping time longer

than for the bollard and so the stopping force would be reduced.

83 Falling objects

1 A falling object is pulled towards the Earth by gravity. This force is called the weight of the object. An object falling through air will experience air resistance. Air resistance depends on the shape of the object and its speed. When the air resistance equals the weight of the object, the object will stop accelerating and move at a steady speed, called its terminal velocity.

2 (a) Initially the parachutist falls at a low speed but accelerates rapidly. When the canopy opens the air resistance increases and so her acceleration is less. As she speeds up her air resistance increases until it balances her weight. She then falls at a steady speed, her terminal velocity.
(b) If the parachutist weighed less, she would need less air resistance to balance her weight, so her terminal velocity would have a lower value.

84 Waves

1 Echoes are due to sound reflected from a hard surface.

2 Refraction can be seen when a ruler is put in water. The ruler appears bent because the light has changed direction as it leaves the water.

3

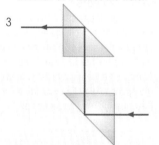

85 Measuring waves

1 Longitudinal waves: sound waves. Transverse waves: light waves, water waves, waves along a rope.

2 Put a cork in some water. Drop a stone into the water. The waves travel out from the centre, making the cork floating on the water move up and down. Although circular waves travel out across the water, the water only

moves up and down, and the cork does not move outwards.

3 330 m/s.

86 Sound and ultrasound

1 Sound travels by vibration being passed from one particle to the next. A vacuum does not contain any particles so there can be no transmission of sound.

2 50 Hz.

3 300 m/s.

4 For example, when you are in the hall you can hear the television, even though you cannot see it. The sound waves are diffracted through the open door. (If the door is closed the sound is much quieter, because it had to pass through the door.)

87 The electromagnetic spectrum

1 X-rays are an ionising radiation and are known to damage living cells; there is no evidence that ultrasound damages cells.

2 Ultraviolet light from the Sun damages cells, which may lead to skin cancer.

3 Infrared is detected by the camera cells, the camera then converts it to an electrical signal and displays it in the visible spectrum.

4 Mobile phones emit microwaves. The phone is held close to the head. Cooking uses other microwave wavelengths.

88 Communications

1 Optical fibres are cheaper to make; they can carry many more signals in the same thickness cable; optical signals need boosting less often.

2 Microwaves can carry much more information and the ground does not have to be dug up to bury cables.

3 Digital signals suffer less from interference and digital signal cables can carry more information.

4 Diffraction.

89 Plate tectonics

1 (a) There may be volcanoes or earthquakes.
   (b) Molten rock rises to the surface forming new plate material.

2 The coastlines of Africa and South America match in shape and the rocks and the fossil records suggest that they were once close together. When new plate material forms it records the direction of the Earth's magnetic field at that time. The patterns give information about the way the plates have formed.

90 Waves through the Earth

1 P waves are longitudinal waves, travel more quickly and can travel through solids, liquids and gases and, therefore, right through the Earth. S waves are transverse, travel more slowly and can only pass through solids. They are not transmitted by the outer core of the Earth.

2 P waves travel more quickly than S waves, so there is a spread of time over which waves arrive. The further the station is from the epicentre the longer the time delay. The delay is longest at a position opposite the epicentre.

91 The Earth and beyond

1 (a) Venus.
   (b) A.
   (c) The path of a comet is a more stretched ellipse, passing way beyond the orbit of planet C.
   (d) The comet moves fastest when it is closest to the Sun.

2 The Moon.

3 Gravity.

92 Our place in the universe

1 Stars are formed when gravity pulls together massive clouds of dust and gas in space, fusing hydrogen nuclei to make helium.

2 The Sun may expand to form a red giant; then contract to a white dwarf.

3 The dust and gases from a supernova may be attracted back together by gravity to eventually form a new star.

93 Energy and work

1 1250 J.

2 (a) 1200 N   (b) 1800 J.

3 (a) 400 000 J   (b) 400 kJ.

Answers

94 Power and efficiency

1 (a) 1600 J   (b) 160 W.
(c) The lift would also need to lift the chair; the lift also has to overcome friction; the lift is not 100% efficient.

2 (a) 600 N   (b) 20 m.
(c) 12 000 J   (d) 67 W.

95 Energy transfers and temperature

1 The pan handle is a good insulator. It prevents the hand being burnt when removing the pan from the stove.
The coat is a good insulator. It prevents heat from the child's body escaping, making her cold.
The tank jacket is a good insulator. It prevents heat escaping from the tank.
The base of the pan is a good conductor. It allows the efficient transmission of heat.

2 (a) Energy is lost by conduction through poor insulation in roofs; energy is lost by conduction through single-glazed windows; energy is lost through draughts, cold air gets in under poorly fitting doors.
(b) Add loft insulation; double- or even triple-glazed windows; fit draught excluders.

96 Potential energy and kinetic energy

1 Aircraft has kinetic and gravitational potential energy, both transferred by the engines from the fuel.
The cyclist has kinetic energy transferred from food.
The book on the shelf has gravitational potential energy transferred by the person who placed it there from food.

2 (a) 0.5 kg   (b) 5 N   (c) 6 J.
(d) 1200 J   (e) 6.7 W.

97 Energy resources

1 Much of the energy has heated the engine and consequently the surroundings; some is used to overcome air resistance, again warming the air around the car; some warmed the road and tyres through friction; some warmed the brakes; eventually all the energy has warmed the surroundings.

2 Only 35% of energy available from coal was used to generate electricity.

3 Wind generators use a renewable energy resource but only work when the wind blows.
Water can be used to drive turbines, it does not pollute but the water supply needs replenishing by rain.

4 (a) A bus can carry 50 people in the road space of 3 cars, which might carry 12 people. The bus will use less fuel and cause less pollution than the three or more cars it replaces.
(b) Less traffic congestion and air pollution
(c) Public transport does not take you door-to-door; it is not as reliable or as convenient as private transport.

98 Radioactivity

1 Charge.

2 Gamma rays; electromagnetic radiation can pass through a vacuum.

3 Two protons and two neutrons.

4 Gamma radiation has a much longer range in air.

5 Alpha radiation would be completely stopped by air; gamma radiation would pass through the paper almost unchanged, but the amount of beta radiation detected would depend on the thickness of the paper.

99 Half-life

1 (a) 6 hours.
(b) Yes.

2 The long half-life means that the uranium-235 will have decayed since the rocks were formed but there will be some left.

100 Uses of radiation

1 (a) Neither alpha radiation nor beta radiation would penetrate to the site of the tumour.
(b) Stops one part of the healthy body being over-exposed to radiation; so the tumour is treated from all sides.

2 The blood carries the iodine to the thyroid where it can work directly; beta radiation would not penetrate the body to reach the thyroid from outside.

A

acceleration the rate at which a moving object is speeding up or slowing down. Measured in metres / second2 (m/s2).

acid substances which produce hydrogen ions when added to water; a pH below 7.

ADH antidiuretic hormone which controls the production of urine in the kidneys.

aerobic respiration During aerobic respiration oxygen is used in the process of transferring energy from glucose in the cells of the body.

alkali metals the elements in group I of the periodic table. They have one electron in the outer shell.

alkalis substances which form hydroxide ions when added to water. Alkalis have a pH greater than 7.

alkenes unsaturated hydrocarbons with a double bond between the carbon atoms.

allele one version of the gene coding for a particular characteristic.

alternating current (a.c.) an electric current which regularly changes size and direction.

amp Electric current is measured in amps. 1 amp = 1 coulomb / second.

amplitude the distance from the crest of a wave to the place where there is no displacement.

anaerobic respiration energy is transferred from glucose without oxygen.

analogue signals carries information by copying the changing pattern of the waves in the original information.

angle of incidence the angle between the direction of a wave and the normal.

artery a blood vessel with a thick muscular wall and a narrow space inside.

atom All elements are made of atoms. Consists of a nucleus containing protons and neutrons surrounded by electrons.

atomic number (Z) the number of protons in the nucleus of the atom.

auxins plant hormones found in the tips of growing shoots and rots. The hormones control the growth of the plant.

B

background radiation We are surrounded by radioactive materials, in rocks, in the air we breathe and particles from outer space. All these sources of radioactive particles are called background radiation.

base metal hydroxides, oxides and carbonates. Bases that dissolve in water are called alkalis.

C

capillary a thin-walled narrow blood vessel.

carbohydrates foods made of carbon, hydrogen and oxygen. They are eaten to supply energy.

carbon cycle shows how the carbon that all living things need for growth is recycled via the carbon dioxide in the atmosphere.

carnivore an animal which eats other animals.

catalyst changes the rate of a chemical reaction without being changed itself.

cell All living things are made of cells, which are the smallest units of living matter. All cells have a nucleus, cytoplasm and a surface membrane.

chlorophyll causes the green colour in plants, necessary for photosynthesis.

chloroplast Plant cells contain chloroplasts which contain the chlorophyll and carry out photosynthesis.

chromosome The cell nucleus contains chromosome pairs which contain many genes.

cloning a process of making an identical copy of a living thing.

combustion the reaction of a substance which is burned in oxygen. Combustion is an oxidation reaction.

compound elements join together to form compounds by forming bonds.

concentration tells us how much of a substance is dissolved in water. Measured in moles per litre or moles per dm3. The higher the concentration, the more particles of the substance present.

condensation molecules in a vapour return to a liquid, losing energy as they do.

conductor An electrical conductor is a

material which allows an electrical current to pass easily. It has a low resistance. A thermal conductor allows thermal energy to be transferred through it easily.

cornea The cornea is the transparent outer coating of the eye.

coulomb (C) measures electric charge.

covalent bond bond between atoms forms when atoms share electrons to achieve a full outer shell of electrons.

cracking the process in which a large molecule is broken into smaller molecules using a catalyst.

critical angle the angle of incidence which results in waves being refracted through 90°.

cytoplasm the living contents of the cell where the chemical processes take place.

D

decomposition a reaction in which substances are broken down, by heat, by electrolysis or by a catalyst.

diffraction happens when waves pass through a gap comparable in size to the wavelength of the wave.

diffusion the effect of randomly moving particles in a liquid or gas gradually spreading from an area of high concentration to one of low concentration.

digestion food passes through the gut and is broken down into small enough molecules to pass into the blood. Undigested food passes out of the anus as solid waste.

digital signal carries information as a series of 1s and 0s which code the values of the original signal.

diode electrical component that only allows electric current to pass in one direction.

direct current (d.c.) always flows in the same direction.

distillation the separation of a mixture into one or more components by evaporation and condensation of the components with the lower boiling points.

DNA the chemical which makes chromosomes.

E

effector part of the body which responds to a stimulus, such as a muscle or gland.

efficiency a measure of how effectively energy is transferred in a system.

electric charge electrons carry a negative charge, protons carry a positive charge. Electric charges attract and repel each other. Electric charge is measured in coulombs (C).

electric current a flow of electric charge around a circuit. Electric current is measured in amps (A).

electrolysis When an electric current passes through a solution or molten solid it is called electrolysis.

electrolyte the liquid which conducts an electric current during electrolysis. It contains ions which carry the current.

electromagnetic induction When a conducting wire moves relative to a magnetic field, a voltage is induced across the wire. This process is called electromagnetic induction.

electromagnetic spectrum a family of waves which all travel at the same speed in a vacuum.

electron a very small negatively charged particle, surrounding the nucleus found in an atom. The number of electrons around the nucleus is the same as the number of protons in the nucleus in a neutral atom.

electronic configuration describes the arrangement of the electrons within the energy levels or shells around the nucleus.

element All atoms of an element have the same atomic number, the same number of protons and electrons and so the same chemical properties.

enzymes made of protein molecules. They are biological catalysts, molecules become temporarily attached to the enzyme during biological processes.

epicentre the place in the earth that an earthquake occurred. Seismic waves spread out from the epicentre.

equilibrium If the rate of the forward reaction and the rate of the back reaction in a reversible reaction are equal the reaction is in equilibrium.

evaporation Molecules near the surface of a liquid may leave the liquid to become a vapour – this is called evaporation.

exhalation (expiration) the process of decreasing the space inside the chest so air pressure rises and air flows out of the lungs.

F

food chain shows the feeding relationship between living things and the way energy and nutrients flow through the system.

food pyramid gives information on the numbers of the different living organisms in a food chain.

food web shows how food chains are interlinked and how organisms in an ecosystem depend on each other.

fossil fuel created over millions of years by the decay and compression of living things, particularly plants.

fractional distillation a mixture of several substances, e.g. crude oil, are distilled; the evaporated components are collected as they condense at different temperatures.

frequency the number of waves produced each second, measured in Hertz (Hz).

fusion During nuclear fusion two small atomic nuclei collide together with such energy that they fuse, releasing energy as electromagnetic waves.

G

galaxy a collection of many stars held together by gravity.

gene a short length of DNA which is the code for a protein. There are many genes within each chromosome.

genetic engineering involves taking genes from one living thing and inserting them into the DNA of another living thing to change its characteristics.

giant lattice compounds formed by ionic bonds form a giant structure in a lattice.

giant structure sometimes covalent bonds produce very strong giant structures.

glucose a simple carbohydrate produced by plants during photosynthesis. Some glucose is used as an energy source by the plant, the rest is converted to starch and stored in the leaves.

gravitational potential energy When an object is lifted against the pull of gravity, energy is transferred to the gravitational field. This is gravitational potential energy.

gravity Gravity is the force which pulls objects to the ground. Gravitational attraction acts between any two objects with mass. The strength of the gravitational field is measured in newtons / kilogram (N/kg).

groups The groups of elements in the periodic table are the elements which have the same number of electrons in their outer shells and so have similar chemical properties. A group of elements lie in the same column in the periodic table.

H

half-life the time it takes for half a quantity of radioactive material to decay to a new substance.

halogens elements in group VII of periodic table with 7 electrons in the outer shell

herbivore an animal which only eats plant material.

hertz measurement of frequency.
1 Hertz (Hz) = 1 per second.

hormone chemicals which help to co-ordinate life processes.

hydrocarbons a group of compounds which contain the elements hydrogen and carbon. Many are derived from oil.

I

igneous rock forms when molten rock cools

inhalation (inspiration) the process of increasing the space inside the chest so that the air pressure drops and air flows in to the lungs.

inherited disease a disease passed on from one generation to the next from the genes of the parents to the child.

insulator An electrical insulator does not allow an electrical current to pass – it has a very high resistance. A thermal insulator does not allow thermal energy to be transferred through it easily.

insulin a hormone involved in the control of

sugar levels in blood.

ion Atoms can lose or gain electrons. When they lose an electron they become a positive ion. When they gain an electron they become a negative ion.

ionic bond forms when an electron is transferred from one atom to the other, forming a positive-negative ion pair.

iris opaque tissue which controls the size of the pupil and so controls the amount of light which can pass into the eye.

isotope atoms of the same element with different numbers of neutrons

J

joule energy is measured in joules.

K

kidney the organ which controls water balance and salt balance and the pH of the blood. Kidneys excrete urea, hormones and medicines in the urine they produce.

kinetic energy on acceleration, energy is transferred to the object. It is energy of a moving object.

L

LDR (light-dependent resistor) resistance value of the component depends on the level of light falling on the component.

longitudinal wave a wave whose oscillations are in the same direction as the energy is travelling.

M

magnetic field A magnetic field is the region in space around a magnet in which other magnets are affected.

mass The mass of an object is a measure of the amount of material in an object. Mass is measured in kilograms (kg).

mass number (A) the number of protons and neutrons in the nucleus of an atom.

meiosis a parent cell divides to create four new sex cells, each with a different combination of chromosomes.

metamorphic rocks formed when rocks are changed by heat or pressure.

microbe small single cell organisms, such as bacteria.

mitosis the process of cell division which results in two identical cells.

monomer a simple molecule.

motor neurone a nerve cell that transmits a signal from the spinal cord to the effector.

mutation a spontaneous change in a gene or chromosome which may result in a change in cells characterised by the gene.

N

negative ion (anion) formed when an atom gains an electron to achieve a full outer shell of electrons.

nephron the structure within the kidney which filters out waste from the blood and allows useful materials to be reabsorbed.

neutralisation the reaction between an acid and a base, producing salts and water.

neutron a small uncharged particle, with the same mass as a proton, found in the nucleus of the atom.

newton measurement of force in newtons (N). 1 newton is the unbalanced force needed to give a mass of 1 kg an acceleration of 1 m/s^2.

nitrogen cycle All living things need nitrogen to make proteins. The nitrogen cycle shows how nitrogen is recycled so it is available to both plants and animals.

noble gases the elements in group 0/VIII of the periodic table, with a full outer shell of electrons and so are unreactive.

normal a line perpendicular to the surface at the point where a wave crosses the surface.

nucleus of a cell made of genetic material such as DNA. The nucleus contains the instructions for the cell.

nucleus of an atom An atom has a small dense positively charged nucleus where most of the mass is concentrated, containing protons and neutrons.

O

oestrogen one of the sex hormones in females which causes puberty.

ohm measurement of electrical resistance.

optic nerve Nerve fibres from the light-sensitive cells on the retina form the optic nerve passing from the eye to the brain.

optical fibres very fine threads of glass through which light can pass, even when the fibre is curved around a corner.

ore a rock containing a mineral which can be extracted from the rock.

osmosis a special case of diffusion – a solvent passes through a membrane from a weak to a stronger solution. The solute cannot pass through the membrane.

oxidation a reaction in which oxygen combines with a substance; a reaction where electrons are removed; a reaction where hydrogen is removed from a substance.

oxygen debt During vigorous exercise anaerobic respiration takes place in muscle tissue. Lactate is produced in the absence of oxygen. When exercise stops oxygen is used to respire the lactate.

P

periodic table lists the elements in order of atomic number. The table is arranged into rows called periods and columns called groups.

periods The periods of elements in the periodic table are the elements in which the same outer shell is being filled up. A period of elements in the periodic table all lie in the same row.

pH The pH scale is a measure of how acid or alkali a solution is. The pH scale runs from 1 to 14.

photosynthesis Plants process water and carbon dioxide to produce glucose by the process of photosynthesis.

plasma the yellow liquid part of blood which contains many dissolved substances.

polymer a large molecule formed from many monomers by polymerisation.

polymerisation the reaction in which many identical monomers are joined together to make a polymer.

positive ion (cation) formed when an atom loses an electron to achieve a full outer shell of electrons.

power the rate at which energy is transferred in a system. Power is measured in watts (W) and kilowatts (kW).
1 W = 1000 kW.

progesterone one of the sex hormones which causes puberty in females.

proteins foods made from carbon, hydrogen and nitrogen. Proteins are used to build enzymes and cytoplasm.

proton a small positive particle found in the nucleus of the atom.

pupil the hole through which light passes into the eye.

R

radioactive decay a random process in which the nucleus of an atom becomes more stable by losing particles and energy.

reactivity series a list of

metals in order of decreasing reactivity. Any metal will displace a metal below it in the Reactivity Series from its solution.

receptor a part of the body which detects a stimulus.

red blood cells contain haemoglobin which transports oxygen to cells and returns carbon dioxide to the lungs.

redox reaction Oxidation and reduction always take place together. The combined reaction is called a redox reaction.

reduction a reaction in which oxygen is removed from a substance; or a reaction where electrons are gained or a reaction where hydrogen is gained by a substance.

reflection Reflection of waves happens when the waves bounce off a surface.

refraction Refraction of waves happens when waves change direction due to a change in speed.

resistance a measure of how difficult it is for an electric current to pass. Resistance is measured in ohms (W).

respiration the process which transfers energy from food to the organism.

retina light-sensitive layer at back of the eye.

reversible reaction chemical reactions which can go both ways. The direction of the reaction depends on the condition of the reactants.

S

satellite a body in orbit

Glossary

BBC GCSE Check and Test: Science

around a planet. Moons are natural satellites. There are many man-made satellites in orbit around the Earth.

saturated compounds atoms are joined together by single bonds.

sedimentary rocks formed when rock fragments are deposited and then pressed together.

seismic waves carry energy away from an earthquake.

sensory neurone a nerve cell which carries a signal from the receptor.

shells of atoms Electrons are grouped within an atom in regions of space called shells or energy levels.

Solar system the Sun, nine planets, the asteroid belt and a number of comets.

speed tells us the rate at which something moves. Speed is measured in metres / second (m/s).

stomata pores (openings) in the surface of the leaf, through which transpiration occurs.

T

temperature regulation The body controls its internal temperature by varying blood flow, sweating and shivering.

terminal velocity When an object moves through a fluid there is resistance to its motion. The faster it travels the greater the resistance. When the driving force is balanced by the resistive forces the object is moving at a maximum speed called its terminal velocity.

testosterone the sex hormone which causes puberty in males.

thermistor an electrical component whose resistance changes with temperature.

total internal reflection occurs when the angle of incidence is greater than the critical angle.

transformer a pair of wire coils linked by a piece of iron. A changing current in one coil creates a changing magnetic field in the iron which causes a changing voltage in the other coil by electromagnetic induction.

transition metals the group of elements in the periodic table between Group II and III.

transpiration the loss of water from a plant by evaporation from stomata.

transverse wave the oscillations are at right angles to the direction in which the energy is travelling.

U

unsaturated compounds one or more bonds between atoms are double bonds.

V

vein a blood vessel with a thinner wall, with a larger space and lower pressure than an artery.

velocity tells us the speed of a moving object and the direction it is moving.

villi The surface of the small intestine is lined with villi, small 'fingers' of gut which increase the surface area for digestion.

volt Electrical potential difference (voltage) is measured in volts. 1 volt = 1 joule / coulomb.

voltage Voltage (potential difference) between two points in a circuit measures the difference in energy carried by the electric charge passing through the circuit. Voltage is measured in volts (V).

W

watt Power is measured in watts (W). 1 watt is 1 joule / second.

wavelength Wavelength is the distance from the crest of one wave to the crest of the next wave.

weight the force of gravity on the object. Weight is measured in newtons (N).

white blood cells fight infection. They make antibodies and overcome bacteria.

work Work is done when a force moves an object. When work is done energy is transferred. Work is measured in joules. When a force of 1 newton acts through 1 metre in the direction of the force, 1 joule of work is done.

Index

Index

Index